Indian Business Case Studies

Indian Business Case Studies

Volume IV

PRITI PACHPANDE
SHAM BACHHAV

Indian Case Studies in Business Management

OXFORD
UNIVERSITY PRESS

OXFORD
UNIVERSITY PRESS

Great Clarendon Street, Oxford, ox2 6dp,
United Kingdom

Oxford University Press is a department of the University of Oxford.
It furthers the University's objective of excellence in research, scholarship,
and education by publishing worldwide. Oxford is a registered trade mark of
Oxford University Press in the UK and in certain other countries

Published in the United States of America by Oxford University Press
198 Madison Avenue, New York, NY 10016, United States of America

British Library Cataloguing in Publication Data

Data available

Library of Congress Control Number: 2022938091

ISBN 978–0–19–286940–1

DOI: 10.1093/oso/9780192869401.001.0001

Printed in India by
Rakmo Press Pvt. Ltd.

Links to third party websites are provided by Oxford in good faith and
for information only. Oxford disclaims any responsibility for the materials
contained in any third party website referenced in this work.

Dr R.R. Pachpande
[1947–2009]

'Education is the Soul of our society'

The series editors and the volume authors of the case volumes titled as 'Indian Business Case Studies' published by Oxford University Press have a deep sense of gratefulness while dedicating these case volumes to the memory of Dr Raghunath R. Pachpande, the Founder of ASM Group of Institutes Pune, India.

It was with the untiring efforts and strategic vision of Dr R.R. (as he was known to his close friends and colleagues) which has been Instrumental in ASM group adopting case methodology as a unique element in its pedagogy which motivated the faculty and students of ASM group of institutes to develop business Case Studies on Indian Businesses and use them to teach management subjects in all branches of Business Management studies.

Dr R.R. Pachpande was a leader beyond parlance and ahead of time in establishing educational institutes more so in higher studies in business Management specifically in the Industrial belts in the state of Maharashtra with a view to providing the best of experiential learning to its students through closer interactions with business Units around.

Today ASM Group continues the great legacy of Dr R.R. Pachpande under the leadership of his successors and who have succeeded in taking ASM Group to global recognition as a unique group of institutes offering world-class education in all branches of Business Management.

This case volume is dedicated to the memories of late Dr R.R. Pachpande.

Contents

Preface   xiii
Acknowledgements   xvii
About the Series Editors   xix
About the Volume Authors   xxi
The How and Why of Case Methodology   xxiii

SECTION I CASE STUDIES IN HUMANRESOURCES

1. A Case on Contract Labour: M/s. Vanita Chemicals Limited   3
   Learning Objectives   3
   Synopsis   3
   The Case Details   4
   Notice   6
   Conclusions   7
   Case Questions   8

2. Maruti's 'Sanjeevani': A Case Study in Long-term IR Issues
   at Maruti Suzuki Ltd—Manesar Plant   9
   Learning Objective   9
   Synopsis   9
   The Case   10
   Insignificant Burden   12
   Social Undercurrents   13
   Conclusions   14
   Case Questions   14

3. Bridging the Skill Gap in the Generation and Technology:
   A Case Study on Cross-generational and Technological
   Change Management Issues   15
   Learning Objectives   15
   Synopsis   15
   Let's Understand the Generation-Based Conflicts   16
   How This Generation Conflicts Co-existed?   16
   Outcome   18
   Future Scenario   19

Conclusions   20
Case Questions   20

4. Motivating through 'Uncertainty': A Case Study in Survival
   Strategy   21
   Synopsis   21
   Case Questions   25

SECTION II CASE STUDIES IN FINANCE MANAGEMENT

5. An Elephantine Exercise: A Case Study on the Mergers of
   Major Banks in SBI   29
   Learning Objectives   29
   Synopsis   29
   Is SBI Biting off More Than It Can Chew?   30
   Size Is the Only Driving Force   31
   Employee Anxieties   32
        A Laggard   33
   The Bad Bank   33
   Weak Core Performance   35
   Conclusions   36
   Case Questions   36

6. Wrong Signals for FDI Climate: A Case Study on
   Retrospective Taxation   37
   Learning Objectives   37
   Synopsis   37
   Operations Strategies   38
   Hutchison Whampoa   39
   Essar   39
   Hutchison Max Telecom Ltd (HMTL)   40
   Case Details   40
   The Supreme Court Verdict   41
   The Underlying Issues Involved   43
   Amendment which Created the Issue   43
   Current Position   44
   Case Questions   45

7. One Nation One Tax: A Case Study on Goods and Services
   Tax (GST) India   47
   Learning Objectives   47
   The Impact and Relevance of the GST Bill   48
   Current Issues   49

Challenges Currently Faced by the Logistic Industry in India 50
Limitations 50
GST: A New Road for Transportation and Logistics Industry
in India 51
Case Questions 52

8. Economics, Markets, Public Life, and Regulators: A Case
Study on Global Economics 53
Learning Objectives 53
Synopsis 53
Case Question 56

SECTION III CASE STUDIES IN MULTIDISCIPLINARY AREAS MARKETING, STRATEGY, OPERATIONS

9. The Candy Lounge: A Live Case Study on a Mexican
Industry on Entrepreneurship 59
Learning Objectives 59
Synopsis 59
The Case Details 60
Organizational Objectives (5–10 Years Plan) 61
The Chosen Business Strategy 61
Market Scenario: Major Competitors 61
Operational Details over Previous Year 2011–2012 61
New Projects Needing Fresh Investments 62
General Information on Batilongo Candy Stores 62
Major Vendor Base (Supply Chain) 63
Manufacturing Strategy 63
Process Choice 63
Modernization Plans and Projects 63
Organizational Capability (Strategic Advantage) Profile 64
Likely Threats in Future for Batilongo Candy Lounge 65
From the Horse's Mouth 65
Conclusions 66
Case Questions 67

10. From Rags to Riches: A Case Study Mexion Wheels
Private Limited India 69
Learning Objectives 69
Synopsis 69
Background of the Company 69
Growth Story 70

Organization Structure: During the Start-up Phase
  There Were Hierarchies of Managerial Levels   70
Production Process   71
Conclusions   74
Case Questions   74

11. Racing to Deliver: A Case Study on E-commerce and
    Logistics   75
  Learning Objectives   75
  Synopsis   75
  The Brick and Click Retail   76
  Same Consumers Online and Offline   76
  Be Present, on Tap   78
  E-commerce an On-Off Affair   78
  Touch and Feel Barriers   79
  Cash on Delivery   80
  In-store Technology   80
  Conclusions   82
  Case Questions   83

12. The Wings on Fire: A Case Study on Tata's Acquisition
    of Air India   85
  Learning Objectives   85
  Synopsis   86
  Case Details: Major Terms of the Deal   87
  The Legacy and Settlement of Outstanding Debts   89
      Air India   89
  The Possible Synergy   90
  Air India to Give Wings to Tata's Aviation Ambitions   90
  On the Table   92
  Major Challenges for the Turnaround   93
  The Tata-Air India   95
      Integration Process Has Already Begun at Tatas   95
  Conclusions   95
  Case Questions   96

13. A Good Strategy for Growth?: A Case Study on Merger of
    Sun Pharma and Ranbaxy   99
  Learning Objectives   99
  Synopsis   99
  Historical Background   100
  Ranbaxy's Legacy   100
  About Sun Pharma   100
  The Synergies   101
  Global Market for Sun-Ranbaxy   101

Detailed Turnaround Plan 102
The Challenges 102
Merger Strategy: An Expert Advice 102
Man Power Planning 103
Operational Strategy 103
Regulatory Strategy 103
Markets after Merger and Acquisition 104
Regulatory Challenges for Being a Monopoly 104
Case Questions 105

14. Transformative Turnaround Strategy: A Case Study on
Mahindra & Mahindra's Successful BPR Exercise 107
Learning Objectives 107
Synopsis 107
The Case Details 107
Conclusions 111
Case Questions 112

15. 'One' versus 'Many': A Case Study on Product Branding 113
Learning Objectives 113
Synopsis 113
The Case Study 114
Choosing My Style 115
Conclusions 118
Case Questions 119

16. E-mobility—From the Current to the Future:
A Case Study in E-automobility 121
Learning Objectives 121
Synopsis 121
The Policy Front 122
Radical Ideas Required 123
The Real Challenges and Barriers to Going Electric 123
Incentives 124
Cost of the Battery 124
Price Multiple 125
Challenges from the Grid Side 125
What Next? 126
Conclusions 127
Case Questions 127

17. What Really Went Wrong with Snapdeal?: A Case Study
on Failure of a Promising E-commerce Start-up 129
Learning Objectives 129
Synopsis 129

Snapdeal Founders Admit Their Mistakes—What Went Wrong? 130
Execution Errors 130
An Imitator in Business 130
Late Entry into Mobile Payments 131
Departure of Senior-level Executives 131
Drop in Its Valuation 132
Struggle in Raising Funds 132
Snapdeal Mass Lay-Offs (Cost-cutting Measures) 133
Snapchat—Confusion Costs against Snapchat 134
Conclusions 134
Case Questions 135

18. The BSNL Saga: A Case Study on the Collapse of BSNL—
The Telecom Company in Public Sector 137
Learning Objectives 137
Synopsis 137
Revival of the Sick? 138
Bridging the Income-Expenditure Gap 140
Conclusions 141
Case Questions 142

19. Future of the 'Future Group': A Case Study on an E-
commerce Retail—The Giant 'Future Group' 143
Learning Objectives 143
Synopsis 143
The Case Study 143
Debt Financing and Restructuring 145
Inconsistent Approach 146
What Next? 147
The Covid-19 Effect 147
How Loan Moratorium and IBC Saved Kishore Biyani from
Debt Crisis 147
Conclusions 148
Case Questions 149

20. ITC at Cross Roads 151
Hotels, Branded Foods 152
Stubbing It Out 153
The Challenges before the New COO 154
Lessons from BAT 155
Case Questions 157

Preface

Many universities and management institutes across the globe have adopted the case study methodology for teaching almost all branches of management studies for several decades. This trend has been seen in India also, wherein the Indian Institutes of Management (IIMs) and progressive management institutes in private sector have implemented case methodology as an important pedagogical tool in business management education.

However, there is a severe shortage in Indian Business Case Studies faced by the B-schools in India and those global institutes associated with Indian academia. Majority of the case studies studied at IIMs and other A-grade B-schools in India are from situations in industries in foreign countries and have very little or no relevance to Indian business situations. This acts as a major gap for faculty and students engagement in business management studies both at UG and at masters level (PG) studies, wherein for clarification of theoretical concepts is possible mainly through use of case methodology which enables insight into business real-life business situations.

Besides, the objectives and purposes for which case studies are developed abroad are much different from course of studies in Indian B-schools. Therefore, the dependence on foreign case studies for Indian students does not provide any real situational insight on Indian business. Although the curriculum requires taking the students through case study methodology, there are not many Indian case studies for this purpose.

The main objectives of using case-based teaching as a major pedagogical tool in B-schools are as follows:

1. To facilitate students' concept development capabilities through exposure to real-life problems in industries.
2. To enable students to correlate theoretical topics with the techniques used in analyzing complex issues in business situations.

3. To develop skills using which students can develop application matrix for the theoretical topics for real-life problem analysis and resolution techniques.

4. Help the students of B-schools to develop orientation towards the important attributes and attitudinal requirements for effective handling of complex situations at the workplace.

5. To develop a clear understanding of the techniques used for problem analysis, situation analysis and decision analysis and appropriate understanding of the difference between problems and situations in management.

6. To develop the group-based approaches to solving problems and challenges at the workplace by appropriate coordination of and collaboration with all related aspects of a situation.

7. To develop a reference manual for recording the problems tackled and the essential lessons learnt from past incidences for use in future eventualities of recurrence of issues.

8. To develop the preventive steps that must be initiated to ensure the problems resolved once do not recur in the immediate future.

Business case studies are basically oriented towards developing the evaluative and analytical skills of students towards industry situations. Such case studies draw the attention of participants of the case resolution methodology on the in-depth correlative evaluation of the issues in the case study with the various related topics that the students have to study about in their classrooms. These case studies could be on issues related to human resources, industrial relations, product and process, marketing and finance management areas in business management.

The academic environment across the world too is facing a major disruption on account of the global pandemic Covid-19 forcing the offline education system to switch over to online/blended versions of teaching and learning process. And use of case methodology and simulation exercises are the main in gradients for sustaining effective ways of delivering experiential learning through use of case and case lets in an online mode of teaching ensuring student engagements and online interactive ways of knowledge dissemination.

Oxford University Press in association with ASM Group of Institutes Pune, India is publishing for the first time comprehensive case volumes as series of eight volumes with case studies on Indian businesses selected from all aspects of business functions like HR, Finance Marketing, and Operations+ providing an exciting and long waited opportunity to faculty and students across the globe to access Indian Business Case Studies through these case volumes.

We are very confident that the case volumes will receive very good response and will be of utmost use to the readers.

Acknowledgements

The series editors and the volume authors wish to acknowledge with thanks the contribution of data for the case studies from ASM's Academic Associates the CETYS University Mexico-Dr Scott Venezia, Dr Francisco Velez, Dean of Colleges Case studies on Candy Lounge, as also several senior faculty from ASM Group of Institutes for their help in proofreading and editing of the case studies.

We also acknowledge the numerous reporters and of daily newspapers in business and economics scenarios in India which have been rich and authentic secondary data sources for design and development of case studies for the case volumes.

About the Series Editors

Dr Sandeep Pachpande, Chairman,
ASM Group of Institutes, Pune, India

Prof J.A. Kulkarni
Professor, ASM Group of Institutes, Pune, India

Both the series editors have decades of experience in business case design and development as also implementation of case methodology of teaching for the faculty and students of business schools in India and abroad.

The series editors have to their credit of authoring three major books on business case studies published by globally known publishers and in conducting workshops for Case design and development.

The series editors have a very good network with leaders and stalwarts in business management studies across the globe and popular as keynote speakers in many national and international conferences. They have a very rich experience in organizing national and international conferences and case competitions.

Currently the series editors are busy completing a unique case analysis and resolution methodology program which is under copyright considerations.

Dr Sandeep Pachpande   **Prof J.A. Kulkarni**

About the Volume Authors

Dr Preeti Pachpande, MBA, Phd

Dr Priti Pachpande is currently one of the ASM Groups' Board of Trustees. Dr Priti Pachpande has 17 years of rich educational and administrative experience and specializes in teaching marketing management subjects for the MBA students.

She has contributed many papers and business case studies in the national and international research conferences and is an expert in case study based teaching methodology.

Dr Sham Bachhav, BE (Elect.), MBA, PhD(Mktg.)

Academic Experience

Dr Sham Bachhav is a university-approved professor in Systems and Marketing and has 21 years of rich experience as a faculty in Operations and Systems Management topics. He is currently engaged as a professor in ASM group of Institutes for the MBA students and also actively involved in various accreditation activities for the institute.

Dr Sham Bacchav has authored and published two text and reference books on operations and supply chain management and has to his credit more than ten research papers presented in National and International Conferences.

Dr Bacchav has authored Case Studies in Operations and Supply chain Management and has adjudicated many case Competitions for Corporates and PG students and faculty.

The How and Why of Case Methodology

An insight into the use of case methodology in B-school pedagogy.

Case Methodology in Business Management Studies

The main objectives of using case-based teaching as a major pedagogical tool in B-schools are as follows:

1. To facilitate students' concept development capabilities through exposure to real-life problems in industries.
2. To enable students to correlate theoretical topics with the techniques used in analysing complex issues in business situations.
3. To develop skills using which students can develop application matrix for the theoretical topics for real-life problem analysis and resolution techniques.
4. Help the students of B-schools to develop orientation towards the important attributes and attitudinal requirements for effective handling of complex situations at the workplace.
5. To develop a clear understanding of the techniques used for problem analysis situation.
6. To analyse decision analysis and appropriate understanding of the difference between problems and situations in management.
7. To develop the group-based approaches to solving problems and challenges at the workplace by appropriate coordination of and collaboration with all related aspects of a situation.
8. To develop a reference manual for recording the problems tackled and the essential lessons learnt from past incidences for use in future eventualities of recurrence of issues.
9. To develop the preventive steps that must be initiated to ensure the problems resolved once do not recur in the immediate future.

Major Types of Case Studies

The entire gamut of business case studies can be classified as follows:

1. Evaluative case studies (teaching case studies)
2. Task- or action-oriented case studies (including project-based case studies)
3. Research-oriented case studies

Evaluative or teaching case studies are basically oriented towards developing the evaluative and analytical skills of students towards industry situations. Such case studies draw the attention of participants of the case resolution methodology on the in-depth correlative evaluation of the issues in the case study with the various related topics that the students have to study about in their classrooms.

These case studies could be on issues related to human resources, industrial relations, product and process, marketing and finance management areas in business management. Such case studies help the students mainly to examine their understanding of evaluative steps such as evaluation of the financial situation of a company or the quality aspects of its products and services, etc.

The task- or action-oriented case studies dwell on business issues that call for appropriate decision-making capabilities of executives. By involving students of management studies in the resolution activity of such case studies, the skills learnt by them through the theoretical studies can be experimented in the resolution exercises. The students can be motivated to apply their decision-making skills along with their risk management ability to make business decisions.

Developing a plan of actions oriented towards the resolution of the case issues calls for effective role-play techniques as also presentation skills from the part of students; they are normally required to defend their plan of approach and decisions in front of other students and the faculty, which helps them improve their capabilities to sustain questions and criticisms, normal features in business management.

Research-based case studies, as the name suggests, involve students in research initiatives to establish a hypothesis or to disprove a common belief, which influences the progress and sustenance of business ideologies or even scientific or technical aspects of business dynamics.

These case studies normally call for prerequisites such as thorough business knowledge and enough exposure to both the theoretical and practical aspects of the issues presented in the case studies. Issues of corporate governance and social welfare functions, which have both obligatory and voluntary elements attached to them, are pursued in research studies to establish the utility purposes of such aspects, which range from free will to a compelled activity.

Market-survey case studies help students to differentiate between facts and fantasies of customer behaviour and understand the competitive forces at play in the marketplace. Business environmental analysis and the study of business options and strategic choices are recommended areas for case studies calling for research.

However, the real problem today for B-schools is the non-availability of good case studies on Indian business. Since the usage of imported case studies from foreign businesses is fast losing its relevance to the Indian business scenario, which in itself has unique features among the global economies. India, which is rated as the world's fourth-largest economy, definitely needs specific and separate approaches to the case study methodology as a pedagogical tool for B-school studies.

This also calls for intensifying the industry-institute interactions at least at the B-school level of education. Both sides need to shed their shy or protective nature to facilitate effective and purposeful interactions.

Even the government, and specifically the department of higher education, needs to emphasize the absolute need for closer contacts between the higher educational institutes and the business houses in all segments of the economy. Only then can the studies at higher level be compatible with the needs of businesses and the educational degrees or qualifications be worthy of any application in the real economic progress of India, based on domestic skills as relevant to business needs.

Case studies in business management are characterized by their relevance to the theories and practices of businesses across the world. While there could be cultural differentiation, the need is to align with the basic purpose of business ventures. Men, machines, and materials form the basic resources of a business, and customers at the relevant marketplace create the necessary turnover of these resources.

Every business or entrepreneurial venture is preceded by the necessity of there being means for survival and creation of wealth by the stakeholders. It is in a way a mixture of needs, actions, and results in a perpetual series and cycle of events, which consume and recreate themselves for the continuity of life on this planet perhaps.

Case Study: Design and Development Methodology

Case studies in business management are characterized by their relevance to the theories and practices of businesses across the world. While there could be cultural differentiation, the need is to align with the basic purpose of business ventures. Men, machines, and materials form the basic resources of a business, and customers at the relevant marketplace create the necessary turnover of these resources.

Every business or entrepreneurial venture is preceded by the necessity of there being means for survival and creation of wealth by the stakeholders. It is in a way a mixture of needs, actions and results in a perpetual series and cycle of events, which consume and recreate themselves for the continuity of life on this planet perhaps.

The case studies in business management depend very much on the 'virtual' nature of their contents, and the actual and real-life demonstration of business situations that they bring to the classroom in business schools help in letting the students correlate the theoretical and practical aspects of business management.

Case studies should generate interest in the minds of students and awake in them a curiosity to understand the contents of a case study and an urge to involve oneself in the case analysis and resolution process. Then only can case studies be called effective tools that translate real-life business scenarios to classroom discussion topics.

The case studies in business management are characterized by features as follows:

1. Fact-based contents and narrations rather than fantasies and fiction.

2. Necessity of an appropriate 'hook effect' in case contents and the chronological presentation of a case.

3. Presence of just enough ambiguity and vagueness in the deliberations of the case.

4. Providing clues and not exact solutions to case issues.

5. Providing specificity in the comparison and correlation of case contents to topics of studies in business management.

Case Study Based on Facts

In order to make a case study present a real-life situation, it should necessarily be based on the facts of a business situation, either a past situation or a concurrent happening in the domestic or international business environment. However, in order to protect an individual's or an organization's business interests, one may, to the maximum extent possible, camouflage the names of individuals, organizations or the exact product and process nomenclatures, besides duly respecting the copyrights of the owners of the references made, if any, in the case contents.

The students of business management definitely desire to feel involved when they have to study, analyze and resolve business case studies; hence, any distortion in the facts, details not confirming to regular business transactions or issues not commonly visualized during the course of their studies tend to deflect their focus and create a sense of artificiality or disinterest in their approach to the case study methodology.

In fact, this is one of the most important reasons why case studies based on industrial situations abroad are of lesser interest to the students of Indian B-schools, since they do not depict real business scenarios in the Indian business environment and are deprived of the cultural relevance so essential to Indian students.

It is also observed that in many case studies, an attempt is made by the authors of the case study to dramatize the narration to such an extent that the seriousness of the topic in relation to business management studies is completely disregarded. And such case studies are remembered by the students for their fun content rather than facts of business life. This has an implied risk in that students may totally miss the objective of the case study methodology of business management studies and consider case studies as irrelevant to business studies' requirements.

A good case study, therefore, should necessarily draw the attention of students to the events and facts normally reported in the business magazines or based on reports appearing in the newspapers, journals, such that the students' natural interests are aroused to know more about the issues involved through case analysis and discussions. Students who are aware of the happenings in the business world around them will be happy to clarify their understanding of the theoretical aspects of their course of management studies by making the best use of case study methodology.

Necessity of 'Hook Effect' in Business Case Studies

For a film to be entertaining and interesting till the last scene, it must capture the imagination of the audience and make them feel as though they are a part of the environment created by the film; similarly, it is necessary that business case studies create a feeling in the students that they are a part of the case study from the beginning to the final resolution. This is the essential hook effect that every case study in business management should strive to achieve.

Mind well that this does not mean the authors should resort to fantasizing about the narration of case contents; the purpose of films is pure entertainment, whereas the purpose of business case studies is to develop a strong sense of attachment of the student towards case contents, as is relevant to their course of studies; it is in their own interests to understand the analysis and resolution process of a particular case study that looks so similar to real-life business situations about which they have some knowledge.

Case studies in business management should provide enough opportunities for conflicts and disagreements, lively discussions and competitive team spirit among the students. The case studies should also generate an interest in the students to look out for additional data from sources such as the Internet and business magazines, balance sheets of companies, etc., to gather further information to help them understand management concepts and prepare them to provide effective analysis and resolutions to the questions raised by the case writer.

Every business executive necessarily suffers much anxiety and related stressful situations in the resolution of day-to-day problems at the workplace. The purpose of business case studies is to simulate an environment that is as real as possible using the case content and analysis and resolution process.

'Ambiguity and Vagueness' in Business Cases

A professional manager often comes across ambiguous and vague situations including discontinuous changes in their day-to-day activities. In fact, these situations incite creative and innovative responses from the managers, leading to ensuring sustainability amidst volatile market forces. If every step is based on logic and must be preplanned or doctored, then perhaps life will not be worth living it.

In the parlance of strategic management, we often talk of change management and of 'discontinuous changes', which defy logic and sense of sequencing of events. The real capability factors for effective business management are the ones that can manage business uncertainties like never before in globalized competitive environments. It is these uncertainties, which are the real ambiguities and vagueness in business management, that the case studies are supposed to imbibe while the students are on the lookout for logical steps in analysis and issue resolution.

Case studies should induce the students to think outside the box for the resolution of issues for a given situation. A case study should not be a drab story from cradle to grave or a reincarnation of business practices, which kills the creative capabilities of students and oversimplifies the challenges faced in effective business management. The case studies should deflect logic-based thinking to change management areas wherein the students are required to play different roles in providing long-term solutions to the issues mentioned in the case studies. Questions such as why, when, how, how much, who, etc., should naturally surface while analysing and resolving case issues.

'Clues' for Case Analysis and Resolution

Providing clues and soft hints along the sequence of events in case study analysis and resolution will enable students to direct their analyses towards the objectives of the case study. It is often the experience that students lose their focus on important aspects of the case study and start drifting towards issues on less critical points.

This is also quite often the case in real-life industry situations wherein the major focus in important discussions gets deflected to trivial issues, resulting in wastage of valuable time, conflicts of interests and escalation of the problem rather than arriving at any resolution. Business case studies should make special attempts to keep the focus of the analysis and resolution methodology oriented on major issues.

This can be done by proper sequencing of events in the case study such that the readers of the case are provided with links to the theme of the case as frequently as required by providing clues to the root causes for the issues and hints to the likely solution or answers to the questions asked by the case writer.

For example, if the case writer wants the students to compare the case issues with 'competitive strategy' situations, then the mention of 'competitive environment' as an often-repeated data or issue in the case study would keep the students focused in their analysis and discussions on, say, the 'competitive advantage matrix', as enumerated by Michel Porter on strategic business management topics.

Similarly, case studies in human resources (HR) should provide clues on HR-related issues, rather than constantly talking about competition and product-related issues. Of course, in the case of case studies in overall operations management including mergers and acquisitions, it would be prudent to provide related clues on each functional area and the respective topics in classroom studies.

Nevertheless, should the clues attempt to mislead the participants, the very belief and credibility of the case study methodology of studies would be destroyed. It is also equally important to note that the clues should only be indicative and not directive in their purpose.

Case Teaching Notes

Case study teaching notes are primarily for the case instructor or the faculty who use the case study methodology for teaching business management topics to students. Following are some of the important aspects of case teaching notes (these are not exclusive in their coverage; the concerned faculty could add, delete or modify the same to make their case teaching process as effective as possible):

Every case presenter should provide students with a brief summary of the case in order to generate initial awareness and prepare the students to study the case as a cursory note or a preamble of their expectations from the analysis and resolution efforts required for the case study.

A list of the main topic and sub-topics intended to be taught through the particular case study needs to be prepared and discussed beforehand by the faculty with the students, in order to ensure there is enough clarity of understanding and expectations from a particular case study.

Reference to important theories such as Maslow's theory, Herz Berg's theory, Michel Porter's model on business competitive and market forces, GE 9 cell model for investment decisions, etc., in any other specialization area of business management studies should be made in a separate 'Focus of Studies' part of the teaching notes and should be shared with the students in advance of case study discussions to enable the students to consolidate their understanding and applicability of a particular theory during the analysis and resolution process of case study discussions.

The teaching notes should also contain corollary topics and references to other aspects of the course of studies, which may not have been covered in the main case content. Additional information about a product, process, or business unit or comparisons with similar real-life situations and relevant market situations, if available with the faculty, is shared with the concerned students; this will help the students to correlate their knowledge with this additional information, which refers to an actual situation.

Every faculty should necessarily collect feedback from the groups or individuals who have studied the case and their comments on the utility of the case study towards their course of business management studies must be noted. This feedback will help the faculty to make necessary improvements in leading the case study by answering certain observations made by the participants.

Every faculty should prepare an assignment case study to be completed by the students, to encourage students to experience the work life through exercises in case study resolutions.

Prevalent Methods for Case Analysis and Resolution

Case study methods used for providing clarity on management concepts mostly focus on either imaginary situations or events based on records of failures or successes in the organizational setup. Besides, the approach for case-studies resolution has often focused merely on 'SWOT' analysis (SWOT stands for strengths, weaknesses, opportunities, and threats involved in a project) of an organization with a lesser degree of focus on failures in areas such as strategic decision making, strategic planning, and compatibility in organizations to strategic approach and implementation. The issues in strategically managed companies basically emanate from weaknesses in strategic thinking and a systematic approach to problem resolution.

As Dr Peter Drucker, the management guru, says: 'Management of many business units are busy resolving yesterday's problems today. And there is hardly any clarity between problems and opportunity.' He continues: 'Business investments for competitive advantage need to focus on investments in opportunities rather than in problems.' It is observed that many business organizations take comfort in handing over to the consultants the real problems of the organization. In the first instance, there is no reason for problems to exist if one is to ensure strategic correction during the implementation of strategies in ongoing or new business ventures.

The consultants, in many cases, help expedite the early death of such businesses with their third-party approach (lack of involvement and commitment) to the issues referred and their practice of extracting hefty charges for their consultancy reports, most of which are vague prescriptions (glorified 'sounds good'—type recommendations) that help boardrooms feel happy that their future is secured.

However, in today's globalized competitive business environment, the top management needs to lay special emphasis on attending present issues, focusing on the resolution of present issues, burying past problems with appropriate strategy implementation, and preparing for the future, which calls for competitive advantage capabilities.

Further, many companies like business process outsourcing (BPO) companies, knowledge process outsourcing (KPO) companies, and multinational companies (MNCs) are under the clutches of the managerial autocratic ('do as we say') approach. This reduces the creativity of their employees, and converts them to mere 'robots' in their attitudes and presentations. Today, from middle school to management studies logic-based computer-aided business planning processes are being emphasized rather than creativity-enhancing involvements that call for human endeavour in attaining success and satisfaction.

Understanding the major working details of any organization entails the collection of relevant data from sources such as present status and past record of organizational health. In majority of cases, we need to analyse the past performance data. As in the case of biological issues, in an organizational life history there are events and episodes that occur as major factors inhibiting the progress or causing the decline of the organization; in such cases, often the management had no clue or controlling authority over the organization to understand the issues or prevent the decline in advance.

Diagnosing these maladies affecting an organization is comparable to a doctor conducting diagnostic investigation into the serious ailments of his or her patient. For serious ailments (excepting epidemics and contagious diseases), all factors and issues that influence the malady are personal habits, malnutrition, hygiene factors, and also immunity factors developed during the past period that are either protective or provocative to health or sickness, respectively.

Case History Details

1. Symptoms: Present and past, as recorded.
2. Historical data: Business past history, including all important factors such as details of promoters, financing, products, prices and marketing.
3. Factors influencing performance:
   a. Congenital factors: Family background (erstwhile business promoters, vision, mission and objectives); any effects of 'success sclerosis' (arrogance due to affluence from past success), or 'points of inflection' as is called in business terms, could be factors that go unrecognized in the present malady.

b. Professionalization and management thoughts on fresh approach, skill building and competence factors: These lead to the restless urge to change over from complacence to competence (in a competitive market situation) or from intolerance to infectivity of people and processes (as compared to the 'we too ran' attitude of the organization in the past).

As in the case of diversification or acquisition and mergers, the issues could result from correct or defective selection of businesses (products and processes) or partners, the necessity to change, consequent changes in management capability, improvement anxiety syndrome, etc.

c. Hurdles in succession planning: The 'Generation Next' may have different value systems (sometimes non-compatible with those of its predecessors) and not have a balanced or matured approach as seen by business observers.

d. Fresh approach to business philosophy, a new vision or mission in light of the changing global economy: Both vertical and horizontal integrations (forward and backward integrations) aid typical expectations of the customers of the emancipated market environment.

f. Inability to tolerate the impact of coexistence of new and old cultures.

The following logical, sequential and important steps help to understand, in a comprehensive manner, analysis and resolutions for a case study of any type of business or industry at both corporate and functional levels:

1. Data collection and segmentation (case details)
2. Discuss issues/dilemmas/problems involved in the case
3. Diagnosis (case analysis): Correlating issues of the case with relevant styles of narration in terms of management terminology, in practical business life and conducting a SWOT analysis if required
4. Case Resolution (issue resolution—resolutions and recommendations)
   a. Short term (intermediate steps): Damage control steps

  b. Long term (back to life): Regaining normal health
  c. Preventive steps (impact of implementing the recommendations)
      (i) Consequent prevention-oriented recommendations
     (ii) Building strategic capabilities in subjects (organization) to
           develop the capability to succeed and develop adequate im-
           munity in case the challenge or malady repeats or has side
           effects in an altogether new dimension
  5. Record of lessons learnt

(a). Appropriate record of cause-and-effect analysis of issues (b). Record
of probability analysis

Serial Number	Case History (Major Details)	Disease (Investigative Observation) Issues (Major) of the Case	Diagnosis (Relevance to Management Terminology)	Treatment		Preventive Measures (Prepared for Consequences If Any)	Lesson Learnt (Case Record for Future Ref-erence)
				short term	long term		

Stages/Areas of Activity	Tools Recommended
Strategy formulation	Vision, mission, objective orientation driver/business drivers/critical success factors
Strategic analysis	Environmental appraisal methods: Direct–indirect Macro–micro External–Internal stake Holders Organizational appraisal methods: SWOT analysis Risk analysis Boston Consultancy Group matrix GE 9 cell model For investment decisions
Strategic options	Acceptability Feasibility Flexibility
Strategic choice	Best choice matrix

	Must/wish drill
Strategic decisions	Decision matrix
	Decision tree
	Short- and long-term impact analyses
Strategy implementation	Operational control method
	Strategic control method
Strategy evaluation	Gap analysis
	Root cause analysis
	Probability factor analysis of present and potential effects
	Corrective steps
	Review progress
	Reconfirm strategic alignment

The case studies included in this **Case Volume IV** are selected diligently to provide a very variety of businesses and issues involved in each of the cases being much different than the other. The chapters cover almost all types and segments of industry and markets providing a very good opportunity for the readers to refer to the aspects explained in this brief note on case methodology and its utility in concept clarification and exposure to experiential learning for the students of B-schools as also to younger business executives up the career ladder.

SECTION I

CASE STUDIES IN HUMAN RESOURCES

HR, Entrepreneurship, CSR, CG, and Sustainability

1. A Case on Contract Labour
2. Maruti's 'Sanjeevani'
3. Bridging the Skill Gap in the Generation and Technology
4. Motivating through 'Uncertainty'

A Case on Contract Labour

M/s. Vanita Chemicals Limited

Learning Objectives

To understand what pitfalls may happen in a labour contract and how to envisage issues before they go out of control. To be able to manage crisis in real life by sensitizing participants towards the sensitive handling of labours and their problems keeping in mind the interest of management and jurisdiction.

Synopsis

This case is about Ms Vanita Chemical Ltd., which is located at Thane— Belapur Road, Maharashtra. The Company is engaged in manufacturing of various chemicals since 1991. The total manpower of the Company is 450. It had provided canteen for the employees and it was running on contract basis. Mr Rama Shetty was a canteen contractor. The canteen contract was registered by the company under The Contract Labour (Regulation and Abolition, 1970). An agreement was also signed by Rama Shetty as a canteen contractor and on behalf of company a factory manager, Mr Kulkarni.

The case focuses on the issues related to making contract labours 'permanent' in the Canteen of Vanita Chemicals Limited. The canteen employees who were on contract, with the pressure of internal union, demanded the management to make them permanent employee of the company. Retaliating, management issued a letter of termination of canteen contract which was delivered to the canteen contractor immediately. The issue was raised to the Labour Commissioner's Office by the canteen

Indian Business Case Studies. Priti Pachpande and Sham Bachhav, Oxford University Press. © ASM Group of Institutes, Pune, India 2022. DOI: 10.1093/oso/9780192869401.003.0001

employees. The canteen employees started giving slogans against the company. Further they used abusive language against the management. They were doing the same activity every day.

The Case Details

Ms Vanita Chemical Ltd. Company is located on Thane Belapur Road, Navi Mumbai. The company is engaged in manufacturing of various chemicals since 1991. In the company labour force is 450, it has provided canteen for the employees and it is running on contract basis. Mr Rama Shetty is a canteen contractor. The canteen contract was registered by the company under Contract Labour (Regulation and Abolition, 1970). An agreement was also signed by Rama Shetty as a canteen contractor and on behalf of company's factory manager Mr Kulkarni.

The said contract was renewed every year and rates of the contract also were renewed every year with the consent of both the parties. In the canteen Mr Shetty had employed about 10 workers and they were provided with uniforms, attractive wages, and accommodation also.

Mr Shetty was having another canteen contract in the neighbouring company and there he had employed about 15 canteen boys. In both the companies, the canteen was running smoothly. After every three months, Mr Shetty was transferring his canteen boys on rotation in both the companies, so that it was not continuity of job in both the companies for the canteen boys. This practice continued for a long time.

In Vanita Chemicals there was internal union headed by one of the local employees Mr Ramesh Bhoir who was also a member of the canteen committee. In the company, the regular timing of the canteen, i.e., opening and closing hours were displayed by the Personnel Manager, Mr Mohite out the canteen and on the notice board of the company. Mr Bhoir being canteen committee member used to visit the canteen very often and was also friendly with the canteen boys. Majority of the employees were with the canteen food and there were very rare complaints about the canteen which were attended by personnel manager Mr Mohite.

In the month of October 1995, Mr Mohite was on his regular round in the company, and he observed that outside the canteen Mr Ramesh Bhoir along with canteen boys was discussing something when they all saw Mr

Mohite coming towards the canteen; immediately they disbursed from canteen area and Mr Ramesh Bhoir alone remained outside the canteen. Mr Mohite ignored him and went back to his office. Mr Ramesh followed him and went to the office of Mr Mohite. He told him that he wanted to discuss with Mr Mohite on a serious problem which was to come in the very near future. Mr Mohite allowed him to come inside the office and asked him about the problem.

Mr Ramesh told Mr Mohite that canteen boys were after him for the last two months asking him to make the entire canteen boys union members, of which he is the president. Further they were demanding that all the canteen boys should be made permanent in the company and for this work they had offered a lump sum amount of Rs 50,000/-. In turn, Mr Mohite asked him what you have decided.

Mr Ramesh told Mr Mohite that being a local worker, he could not do such favour to the canteen boys because the canteen boys were from Karnataka, and management would also not agree to this so he thought to inform Mr Mohite because an indirect hint was given by canteen boys to Mr Ramesh, that if he could not do this favour for them, they may join outside the union and put pressure on management for making them permanent. Mr Mohite asked Mr Ramesh what have you promised them?

Mr Ramesh said that he has asked them to wait for 2–3 days so that he could discuss the matter with his other committee members. Up till now I have not talked to the committee and first time I have come to inform you that it is serious matter and management should do something immediately so that our relation should be maintained harmonious like past years. Further, he added that he is not going to accept any money from canteen boys and decided to cooperate with the management.

Immediately after the departure of Mr Ramesh, the personnel manager went to the works manager's cabin and narrated the problem which is likely to be faced by the management. Both of them agreed that it is never be possible to make contract workers permanent in the company; because excess workers in helper's category are employed through union and local politicians. It is going to be a big problem for the company. Both of them called the canteen contractor Mr Shetty immediately and he was asked about whether he was aware of the above fact. He said no. But he would try to convince his workers and asked for one day's time only.

The next day Mr Shetty was busy with his personal work and did not come to the factory. Mr Mohite along with works manager and other departmental heads called a meeting about the issue of canteen boys and finally it was decided to terminate the canteen contract with immediate effect and to ask Mr Shetty to take away his men and material along with compensation whatever is due to him. Mr Mohite again called Mr Ramesh Bhoir and union committee members and appreciated the committee members and work done by Mr Ramesh. Being a union president and disclosed the decision of the management and read out the draft of the notice which was to be displayed on the notice board which was as under:

Notice

'All employees are hereby informed that due to unavoidable circumstances the canteen will not be running from tomorrow from the First Shift till further arrangement will be made. Meanwhile, all employees will be supplied with snacks and tea from outside. All are requested to bear with the management for further few days.'

Mr Ramesh told all the committee members about the problem of canteen boys and decided to cooperate with the management and not to interfere in the matter of canteen issue. After all agreed, finally the notice was displayed on the notice board of the company by the Management.

A letter of termination of canteen contract was delivered to Mr Rama Shetty who was present in the neighbouring company where he was having the contract, through the security. An acknowledgement of the said letter was received back by the personnel manager, Mr Mohite. Accordingly, in the same night, security men were instructed by the personnel manager to remove all the canteen boys and not to allow them to come inside the factory premises with immediate effect. The action was taken by Security Department immediately.

Here, the matter was not closed. Keeping one day gap, canteen boys approached to another union leader of that local area. The union was called 'Maharashtra Sramik Sena' of which Mr Ashok Mahatre from Turbhe area was vice president of the union having office at Turbhe village. The canteen boys become the members of that union and went to Labour Commissioner Office, Thane along with Mr Mahatre. They complained and demanded that the temporary workers who were working for more than three years in the canteen as helpers were removed by Ms Vanita Chemical Ltd. Hence, they should be given justice by Government with reinstatement with full wages and continuity of service and Labour Commissioner Office should take immediate action against the management of Ms Vanita Chemical Ltd.

Because of pressure from local leaders Mr Mahatre, the Labour Commissioner Office accepted their letter of complaint and orally told them that action will be taken against company within few days, till that time, the removed workers and union should maintain discipline.

Thereafter, the next day, Mr Mahatre along with canteen boys and other local people approached the company's gate along with the copy of the letter which was submitted in the Labour Commissioner's Office. The mob was about 35–40 and they handed over the said letter to the security personnel which was sent to the personnel manager, Mr Mohite.

Mr Mohite came at the gate, he narrated the fact to the union leader, Mr Mahatre and for further discussion as and when he will be called by Labour Commissioner's Office then only matter will be discussed and meanwhile not to create any problem at the gate of the company and he went back to his office.

Mr Mahatre and others at the same time started giving slogans against the company and further they used abusive language against the management. Every day in the morning, they used to gather at the gate and were giving slogans. They were doing the same activity every day. It continued for further eight days.

Thereafter, management received a letter from the Labour Commissioner Office, Thane and called for Conciliation by Assistant Labour Commissioner, Mr Pawar who was to handle this matter. Hence, the conciliation started endlessly. Further, the matter went to Labour Court. Meanwhile, all the canteen boys without getting any justice left the union and the matter was remained unsolved in Labour Court.

Conclusions

This case is to shed light on issues related to making contract labours 'permanent' in organizations. The Government of India enacted the Contract

Labour (Regulation and Abolition) Act 1970 in order to regulate establishments wherein contract labour has been employed by the contractors. The Act regulates that the contractors or principal employer have to provide and maintain the health, safety, and welfare of contract labours.

A Central and State Advisory Board has also been formed in order to implement the provisions of the Act. Through the experience of the canteen of Vanita Chemicals Limited, post the enactment of the Act, the case tries to elucidate the roles and jurisdictions of the union, the management and the canteen contractor and how unorganized unionism can lead to fruitless wastage of time and productivity.

Case Questions

1. The issue of engaging contract labour has given rise to many IR issues over the previous years including the one at Maruti Udyog. The validity and legality of employing contract labour is questioned by experts in Labour Law and the Ministry of Industry and labour is hoodwinking this issue perhaps because the Government itself is the largest employer of contract labour in India. Under circumstances how would go about finding a long-term solution to this issue?

2. In the referred case the issue of contract labour has been taken further beyond the scope of definition of principle employer, and the employees of the canteen contractor are trying to disturb the IR climate inside the premises of an organization other than the principle employer—How could one get over such tricky situation?

2

Maruti's 'Sanjeevani'

A Case Study in Long-term IR Issues at Maruti Suzuki Ltd—Manesar Plant

Learning Objective

The primary objective of this case study is to give business, social, and historical perspective of the reasons behind the series of incidents that took place at the Manesar plant of Maruti Udyog Limited in 2012 which led to the murder of a senior HR executive and extensive damage to property.

The secondary objective of this case study is to highlight the future implications of the unpleasant incidents which took place at Maruti Udyog Limited and to encourage the reader to think of the further effects of the same in the industrial relations and business scenario in India from the long-term point of view.

Synopsis

Maruti Suzuki, a leader in car production in India, has often faced troubles with agitation of workers. It has two plants, one in Gurgaon and another in Manesar both located in Haryana. The protest by workers at Maruti Manesar plant turned violent on 18 July 2012. Some 300 workers entered the premises, used rods, tools, and anything which they could grab to attack supervisors and managers. They bet them mercilessly and put the premises on fire. About 100 employees were severely injured and one senior HR manager Mr Awanish Kumar Dev was literally crippled and charred to death. The attack by workers was the worst of its kind and that too it happened in a place which is barely 45 km from NCR region. The incident shocked the whole nation and it is difficult to understand that

Indian Business Case Studies. Priti Pachpande and Sham Bachhav, Oxford University Press. © ASM Group of Institutes, Pune, India 2022. DOI: 10.1093/oso/9780192869401.003.0002

agitation can turn so violent in this century where host of mechanisms are available to amicably solve the issues between management and workers. A few days prior to this incident one supervisor made casteist remarks to one of the workers. The worker slapped the supervisor. Management took swift action and removed the worker from service. The workers were agitating for induction of this employee and wanted to know why no action had been taken against the supervisor. This combined with some other simmering issues led to violent attack by workers on that fateful day. The incident at Maruti is an eye-opener and the similar problems lie in many companies which may trigger similar incidents.

The incident of mass violence also speaks about the demand of equal pay for equal work. In addition the rise in living cost, trend of consumerism, and the vast salary gap between senior managers and workers is cause of growing tension and frustration in youth.

There is an urgent need to reform labour laws and professional bodies must put the concerted pressure on central as well as state governments to do the reforms in time bound manner.

India is a growing economy and growth can be sustained only through industrial harmony and peace. The issue must be addressed to entire spectrum of stakeholders, be it the government, HR bodies, corporate unions, student fraternity global investors, etc. We do need a permanent and long-term systemic solutions where discords are handled with dignity and resolutions are found for even most complicated problem.

The Case

In the worst outbreak of labour violence in Maruti Suzuki's 29-year history, a senior human resource executive was killed and scores of officers injured at the company's factory at Manesar in Haryana on 18 July 2012. Soon thereafter, the company dismissed a third of its regular workforce at the unit, declared an indefinite lockout (it was lifted a month later) and, in its single-largest human resource initiative, announced it would stop hiring contract workers. Till then, these contract workers made up a significant portion of the company's total workforce across its factories at Gurgaon and Manesar. The charge sheet filed by the Special Investigation Team constituted by the Haryana government in October 2012, which said that the violence was not influenced from outside but stemmed from internal issues between the workers and the management. Maruti Suzuki has refused to comment on the findings of the investigation but has taken a few measures to ensure that labour unrest does not recur at its factories.

For one, the company has undertaken a programme to regularize all contract workers engaged in core production activities across its five factories in Gurgaon and Manesar. The trouble in all the strikes has emanated from the contract workers who get paid lesser than regular employees, don't get social security benefits and depend on the whims and fancies of the manpower contractors for their livelihood. While the screening and critical examination procedures for the 1,870 contract workers at Manesar (who worked at the factory prior to the incident on 18 July 2012) are underway, the regularization of contract workers at Gurgaon have commence around March 2013. The entire recruitment process is now routed through the company's own human resource department. In the new dispensation, manpower contractors will not be in the picture at all. According to the plan, Maruti Suzuki will have a workforce of 4,500 at Manesar by the end of December 2012. In fact, daily production at the unit has increased by 15% to 1,950 vehicles from 1,700 vehicles rolled out before 18 July.

The company had previously been taking a large number of workers from contractors on a casual basis to meet cyclical demand of the car industry. These workers can be offloaded during the lean months and can be re-hired when the demand picks up. That's because the country's inflexible labour laws make it impossible to adjust the regular workforce in tune with the ups and downs of the market. 'Contract workers are used largely because companies require flexibility,' Maruti's Chief Operating Officer (administration) S Y Siddiqui says. 'Business has become so competitive that industry has stumbled upon this per force.'

Two, the company has increased wages by a record 50% for permanent workers at its Manesar and Gurgaon facilities. Gross salary has been increased by Rs 14,800 per month spread over a period of three years for these workers. While they will get 75% of the increment in the first year, 12.5% each will come in the second and third years. 'We are working out increments for technicians as well', Siddiqui had said at the time of inking the wage pact with the workers. The gross salary of an entry-level worker in the company was Rs 23,500 per month. According to the new wage structure, the average entry-level salary will increase to Rs 37,800 per month over the next three years. For an experienced worker at Gurgaon and Manesar, the increased salary will stand at Rs 51,800 and Rs 39,800, respectively. The wage pact had benefited around 2,800 workers at Gurgaon and around 700 workers at Manesar. Besides, the company has offered an additional Rs 1,000 in an ad hoc payment to workers, travel allowance of Rs 1200 every month, interest-free personal loans of up to Rs 20,000, and doubled insurance coverage to Rs 5,500. Dearness allowance has been made variable so that it will take into account all inflationary pressures. The revision is considered to be very healthy, considering that the company had given an increment of Rs 9,300 per month when wages were revised last in 2009.

Insignificant Burden

Despite the handsome increment offered by Maruti Suzuki in the new wage agreement, the company's wage bill is expected to remain the lowest among listed automobile companies. The company's wage bill is expected to increase by Rs 65–70 crore per annum because of the increments. Maruti Suzuki Chief Financial Officer Ajay Sheth had informed recently, 'Because of the settlement and regularization of contract workers, the wage bill will increase by 0.15–0.3 per cent of the net sales over the next two year'. According to estimates available with industry experts, Maruti Suzuki reported employee benefits of Rs 843.8 crore in the financial year 2011–12, which amounted to 2.4% of the company's net sales. It is also worth noting that Maruti Suzuki has chosen Gujarat for its expansion in the future. Though the company has denied it, there has been speculation that the widespread labour unrest in the Gurgaon-Manesar industrial belt could have played a role in this decision. Maruti Suzuki did not comment on this. In the four instances of labour unrest that Maruti Suzuki has had to grapple with in the course of about a year since June 2011, the company has lost production of around 150,000 units. To put the number in perspective, Toyota had sold 160,000-odd units in the country in the last financial year. Industry estimates suggest that the company has incurred revenue losses to the tune of Rs 5,000 crore.

While the regularization of contract workers and the wage increments may serve to ease out strains in industrial relations within the company, some concerns remain. Says Deepesh Rathore, managing director, HIS Automotive India, a consultancy firm, 'Wage increments should be given to as many eligible workers as possible because financially it does not make a big dent in the profitability of a car maker; but a plant shutdown is a big setback which results in significant revenue losses. But if there continues to remain a significant disparity between the wages of temporary and permanent workers in the company, there is bound to be differences in the workforce.'

Social Undercurrents

Rathore explains that labour problem of the magnitude that was witnessed at Maruti Suzuki occurs due to the confluence of a variety of complex issues ranging from disparities in socio-economic living conditions within the same workforce to lack of identification with a company's work philosophy. 'When a large number of contract or temporary workers within a company get paid a fraction of the salary earned by permanent workers, differences surface within the workforce'. The living conditions of this section of workers are miserable, particularly when contrasted with the socio-economic parameters in the Gurgaon-Manesar region which has developed into one of the country's flagship industrial sectors. Besides, the worker may not be able to identify with the strict work culture of a Japanese company or there could be a complete lack of communication between the management and those on the shop-floor. All these issues need to be looked at.

Amitava Ghosh, senior vice-president and head (regulatory), Team Lease Services, India's largest human resource services company, says, 'If Maruti Suzuki plans to sustain its operations in Manesar under such a volatile and perturbed environment, it should immediately form a committee where heads of local Gram Panchayats must be given a vital role. Also, some part of the activities should immediately be earmarked where female employees can be engaged. More the proportion of female worker less would be the chances of violation ... It's all about trust building in the locality which may work as a great preventer of violence in near future.'

Conclusions

This entire case presents a strong reason for HR executives to increase their involvement at the floor level with the workers in addition to pursuing their professional education and career development. As a part of the initial training for the junior manager while joining service, it is important to make it a part of study the nature of an average worker, their social structure, the previous history of union activities, the study of resolutions and decisions taken and the comparison of the facilities given to the worker vis-a-vis the workers of the competitors.

The present peace at Maruti Udyog, Manesar is a brokered peace between the Haryana Govt and the Maruti management. This certainly is not going to be a permanent solution. As mentioned earlier, an average Haryanvi worker is a hard fighter and it is pointless for the management to encourage, develop, and nurture anti-labour stance among their executives.

Communication of intention at all levels plays an important role in reducing trust deficit. Rather than the unions coming to know about their company's expansion plans through rumours, newspaper or the television, it is in the interest of the company that the management takes the union into confidence about their establishing new facilities in Gujarat or elsewhere. This will go a long way in building confidence among the workers about the honesty and forthrightness of the management.

Case Questions

1. Looking at the sequence of steps taken and the response from the workmen do you think Maruti has resolved all IR Issues?

2. Under circumstances Maruti has altogether new issues at market place. Do you think Maruti needs to review its Product and IR Strategy in India for long-term sustenance and business growth?

3. Was there need to give a look on wage agreement offered by Maruti Suzuki?

3

Bridging the Skill Gap in the Generation and Technology

A Case Study on Cross-generational and Technological Change Management Issues

Learning Objectives

To identify the views, outlook, and perspectives of younger generation that are in contrast to the previous generations. They are highly tech-enabled and prefer texting rather than talking. They are very inventive and innovative and enjoy challenging the status quo. To find the difference between the three generation in time management and demand in work-life balance. Generation views towards the organizational development change and empowerment strategies. Adapting the change from manual to digitalization. Emerging into AI and Industry 4.0 and its challenges.

Synopsis

As the dynamics of the workplace have changed with the evolution of technology, the change in generations has also impacted the organizational fabric. Organizations today comprise three distinct generations with different mindsets, aspirations, and ethos. Generation X consists of those born between 1961 and 1980, while generation Y consists of millennials, that is, those born between1981 and 1995. The youngest is the Gen Z comprising people born between 1996 and 2010. In India,

Indian Business Case Studies. Priti Pachpande and Sham Bachhav, Oxford University Press. © ASM Group of Institutes, Pune, India 2022. DOI: 10.1093/oso/9780192869401.003.0003

millennial account for nearly half of the working-age population, whereas Gen Z has just made its entry.

Let's Understand the Generation-Based Conflicts

Some thought leaders in the HR industry feel it's the skill gap and the psyche of the previous generations, which lead to interpersonal issues at the workplace. 'Nowadays, it's not about re skilling but rather about acquiring a new skill set altogether that creates a difference. The older generation is trapped in their own thinking that poses a challenge to learning new skill.'

For instance, in the manufacturing industry, someone who has spent relatively 10–15 years with one technology may suddenly become redundant. The previous experience can become a roadblock in the adoption of the new technology, which can lead to ego hassles. Today, employees get promoted much early and don't hold the same position for more than three years on an average. The newer generation is expressive, liberal, demanding and will not compromise easily with their expectations, which may also lead to confrontations. They are more open to discussing career issues and choices; they voice concerns; and look for wider purpose in their actions.

The major disconnect occurs when seniors don't realize this and become rigid in their style. There has to be a realization that the style of management which worked 20 years back will not work now. 'Loyalty may not matter for newer generations, but the same cannot be confused with commitment—they are committed till they are with you'.

How This Generation Conflicts Co-existed?

Every generation has its own set of problems and the previous generation has to be considerate about them. The issues arising out of multi-generation workforces become more evident and dysfunctional when one chooses to ignore. The best way to address issues is to connect with different stakeholders on a continuous basis, get a pulse, understand, and act on issues bothering them.

It is important to set the expectations of the generation right and moderate them. Each generation has a role to play for the next generation and the need to mentor, coach, and invest time to build the people and team, the leaders will fall short in time, and hence, Gen Y has to reciprocate the same support received from the previous generation to diffuse any conflicts at the workplace.

The issues arising out of multi-generation workforces become more evident and dysfunctional when one chooses to ignore. 'The best way to address issues is to connect with different stakeholders on a continuous basis, get a pulse, understand and act on issues bothering them.' To manage the generational differences, the organizations can create a positive culture and policies, which are tuned to their demands.

Flexibility is the key to managing people today, but at the same time the manager has to clearly spell out the outcomes and deliverables. There is no harm in having an open discussion with the previous generation. They need help to unlearn the previous skills and get equipped to adapt to new skills. The best way for organizations to deal with such a diverse workforce is to make them realize that they have to respect and provide space to each other.

There should be provisions to create 'life at work'. For instance, if employees have to work for 12–15 hours a day, the organization can intersperse these hours with fitness activities, such as yoga, gym, or coffee hours to socialize, so that these employees can live other aspects of their life. It is obvious that the demography of our workforce will move to include Gen Y and beyond. Organizations will no longer have a choice but to make the workplace congenial, which suits this shift.

Challenges faced by HR/ER, in adapting the digital technology-based operations were one of the main reasons for conflicts arising between the employees from different generations.

The challenges for HR will be to understand how technology blends with the human workforce. It's a great time where AI and other technology frees us up from the administrative low-value jobs and allows talent to up-skill themselves. It is difficult to believe that machines will ever replace the creativity, imaginations, and ideations that humans do. It will be a man and machine world where we use technology to add more value to our work and to the meaning of what we do.

How can technology improve the way HR approaches talent? What we are looking at is how we use AI and data to really understand our people. You get to really understand a talent as a wholesome person with the insights you can draw from AI and data. It's no longer about particular skills but what drives them, what's the psychometrics behind them. 'What really drives the productivity and the bottom line of any organization is known when you understand people that much better, they will be more engaged and deliver a lot more.'

The insights AI can provide ranges from recruitment to development to team dynamics. If you don't understand your people you will always see a conflict in the workplace. If you really go to the level of understanding human behaviours and why they do what they do, what is in their nature, characteristics and life stories that shape them, it changes your perspective as well. It gives a lot more flavour to working relationships as well.

How then is HR evolving as a department along with industry 4.0?

HR teams need to get better at communicating their goals. When you talk about HR policies or practices, you can't speak from a language of governance or policing. You have to change the tone for the business to understand what is in it for them. It's about achieving that sweet spot between meeting employees' demands to the organization's ones. Sometimes when we make a policy or practice, it's really for the greater good but it's never communicated that way. The objective is to explain why we do this, what the end game in mind is. When that starts to happen people will be much more accepting and understanding.

Outcome

- Now it's about humanizing HR because traditionally it has always been from administrative, governance and policing approach and that is changing. We have to change otherwise we won't retain the best talent.
- Another priority is people, more specifically, how we now change the mindset of people behaving in a different world. 'Our world is more agile therefore we have to be more empowered and enabled. We also can't have a one-size-fits-all approach to policies and practices. We can have a certain base but different aspects will need to change.'

- The approach of HR has mostly been mechanical, for example saying what's the policy we need to change and what's the system, we need to change. Now we are flipping that and saying what's the experience that we really want to create? And that experience will then drive the philosophy which will in turn drive the systems we want in place.
- In regard to methodologies the team have begun to adopt a 'Design Thinking' approach for HR transformation. The beauty of design thinking is it's really coming from looking through the customer's lens. The customers in the context of HR are the employees traditionally it's been about solving HR's pain points but the right approach should be about eliminating employees' pain points, or the business as a whole. By using design thinking, you approach the problems from a different lens and therefore get very different outcomes and solutions. It's the people solutions we need to solve.
- Design thinking is about going into a deeper level of 'Critical Thinking' and finding the root cause. It can change HR itself because it's a completely new way of doing things. The benefit of a design thinking approach is that solution turnaround is quicker. With design thinking, the approach is sprint-led. It's an iterative process. There's also a behavioural change as it will not be perfect the first-time round. Look at start-ups for inspiration to implement design thinking. When know how they can churn things out really quickly? And they adopt design thinking, sprints and iterative methodologies that could start changing the thinking itself?

Future Scenario

- Adapting the change in emerging technologies.
- Developing design sprints were a lot of solutions that can be user friendly to adopt.
- There were both quick wins and ones which will need a bit more time to implement. The other key area is filling and matching talent. We should build in-house algorithms to help with matching. Build prototypes for top talent and using it to see how one can scale it up for the organization.

Conclusions

- As HR teams look to radically transform to adapt to a new working culture, they will evolve over the next few years.
- HR will become the advisory and consultant roles for the organization.
- A lot of the transactional jobs will be digitalized which will free up HR to focus on higher value work.
- There will be a self-driven culture, not waiting for HR to tell you what training to go on but to be proactive on what you want to learn leaving HR to fulfil the consultancy role.
- HR is one of the departments most affected by generation gap, digitalization as well as what technology and tools to implement; the question is how the very nature of HR teams will transform?

Case Questions

1. How do you think the organizations could afford an HR/ER activity, effectively managing the paradox of generation and technology gaps?

2. How could one make HR/ER job to be innovative and contributively and enjoyable at the same time?

3. How can modern HR/ER iron out the distresses while themselves being a part of the system?

4

Motivating through 'Uncertainty'

A Case Study in Survival Strategy

Synopsis

'As a result of the 2G spectrum scam, Uninor faces an uncertain future. Will it stay in business after August 2012? Who knows?'

It's a hot afternoon. The swanky cement and glass buildings that define Gurgaon's skyline look ready to melt in the heat. That's perhaps why the air-conditioning at Uninor's office has been turned to maximum cool.

A few hundred employees, men and women, most of them less than 35 years old, are gathered in this open office. There are no cabins, no high walls to hide behind. It is time for Uninor Managing Director Sigwe Brekke's weekly town-hall meeting with his employees.

The MC starts by cracking a few jokes. People around him laugh whole-heartedly, without any evidence of nervousness. Then Brekke takes the mike. He tells his employees, who include a fair population of foreigners, about his meetings with top Indian ministers and his conversations with the Telenor board (it owns two-thirds of Uninor, while one-third is owned by Unitech) in Norway. After speaking for about 20 minutes, he throws the floor open for questions. There are only three. He then asks his employees what their level of confidence is, on a scale of one to ten. The answers are between five and seven. 'Good that you are not zero and good that you are not ten,' Brekke says. He ends with the war cry of Halla bol!

Brekke puts his own confidence level at six. Not without reason. Uninor was perhaps the most serious new telecom operator in India. It has to date got over 45 million customers, and has more than 17,000 employees, over 2,000 distributors, close to half a million retailers, etc. Now, according to the Supreme Court verdict on the 2G spectrum scam, it has to surrender its spectrum by August. The only way out is if the Department of

Indian Business Case Studies. Priti Pachpande and Sham Bachhav, Oxford University Press. © ASM Group of Institutes, Pune, India 2022. DOI: 10.1093/oso/9780192869401.003.0004

Telecommunications, or DoT, auctions spectrum before that. This will be difficult, says DoT.

But Uninor says it can be done—the template is ready from the 3G-spectrum auction of last year. And India is important if Telenor wants to become a player of global significance. Already, Uninor contributes the maximum number of subscribers to Telenor.

So Brekke is working at various ends: lobbying with the government to auction the spectrum quickly but not to price it exorbitantly, negotiating with new investors, telling business partners it's not yet over, and holding on to his people.

Brekke says that he is so overwhelmed by the energy and spirit of Uninor's employees in this difficult time that, although a question mark hangs over its future, the company has given them 'one month's salary as bonus'. They also got a respectable 12–13% increment in April. 'There was always transparent communication from the management. Since this crisis broke out, the open flow of information has only increased,' says an official from the sales department who has been with Uninor from the beginning, in 2008 Brekke gives no false hope to the employees. He tells it like it is. There may have been no exodus, but some employees have left, and some are looking out for offers, he says. 'The top ones have stuck on,' he adds.

Rival operators know this is the ideal time to poach. Uninor employees now frequently get SMSs such as this one from rival operators: 'Interviews for sales positions across West UP ... Please come with your CV.' Not many seem to be taking the bait.

Keeping workforce morale high is only one part of the exercise. Outside office, the employees also have to explain to their spouses, parents, and perhaps even children why they are sticking with a company which may well have no future in India. Brekke has taken upon himself this task as well. He has written to the families of every employee and also met several of them.

'At one such meeting a woman told him how worried she was because not only did her husband have to feed the family, he also had a monthly loan to repay,' says an official from the operations department. 'Brekke somehow manages to draw people out, give them the real picture no matter how grim it is and yet take them along with him,' says the employee who, incidentally is no fresher in the industry but a man in his late 30s and with enough experience with various telecom operators to know that ordinarily a management's assurances are to be taken with a fistful of salt. 'What's happening here is anything but ordinary,' he says.

The employees may be charged up but they have plenty of questions. Not only do they raise them at the weekly meetings, they also email their concerns to Brekke, who responds to them in an in-house recorded video interview titled 'Hard Talk'. The employees can access the interview on the organization's intranet which these days also has 'I love Uninor', 'We are with you Uninor', and 'Hang in there Uninor' messages with pictures pouring in from Telenor employees across the globe.

One employee asks: Is it true that Uninor and India are out of Telenor's forecast? 'That's true,' says Brekke, without beating around the bush. 'And it's because of the uncertainties surrounding Uninor at the moment, though Telenor has every intention of staying on and would want to increase its equity to 74 per cent with the new partner.'

This triggers another question: Has Telenor found a new partner? Brekke responds, 'You know we need to separate from our current wife [Unitech]. We need to find a new one. We are talking to five or six and all are beautiful.' Laughter goes up in the room.

Employees are confident that if Telenor remerges in a new avatar, each one of them will find a place in the new company. Assets and customers, too, will be transferred.

Telenor, Brekke later tells us, will want to run the show. It is looking for a partner who has an economic interest. All he's willing to reveal at this point is that the partner will not be another telecom player. Could it be a real estate giant like Unitech, with which Telenor fell out after the 2G scam? Uninor having been bitten once, Brekke lets the question pass with a smile.

Out in the market, where rivals have gone into overdrive to snatch business from Uninor, the challenges are altogether different. One poster in Bihar, clearly posted by a rival, reads: 'Caution!! Country's highest institution, Supreme Court of India, has cancelled licenses of S-tel, Uninor and MTS in Bihar and Jharkhand circle. Please do not get misguided and stay alert.' An SMS from another rival to its employees goes: 'Start doing MNP [Mobile Number Portability] drive. Team kindly carry today's [news] headline on 'Telenor threatening to pull out of India if TRAI proposals r accepted' to each outlet. This has to be done to dump its acquisition. Follow it in spirit.'

Brekke knows what's happening. 'Every day, or every other day, our sales staff is physically visiting practically every Uninor retailer. The big ones we're visiting several times a day,' says Brekke, who has also written to every sales partner. 'Constant dialogue is also on with our distributors.'

A Uninor poster in the office of Rajeev Kumar, a territorial sales manager, or field officer, in Bangalore, reads: 'We invested Rs 14,000 crore and won 4 crore customers in the process. That's why we are committed to staying in India.' The posters were distributed to employees a couple of months ago, says Kumar, in what seems to be an attempt to shore up confidence. Kumar, who has been with Uninor for three years, since before its services were rolled out, knows the hurdles the company faces but is confident it will bid again for the licences.

Kumar is also reassured by the fact that the company is still hiring. 'If it really had plans to exit, the first step would be to fire employees,' he says. The company's growing subscriber base, despite the wrangling over licences, is another source of comfort.

Kumar has a team of two distributors, each of whom is responsible for supplying to 300–400 outlets. He has a target of 1,800 connections a month, which he says he is able to meet. 'Many customers these days have two numbers, one a personal number and another for business, which will usually have very low tariffs. Uninor is able to target the latter category,' says Kumar, who himself uses his Uninor number for business calls, while retaining his Airtel number for personal calls.

The field officer admits he's a bit anxious about what the future holds. 'We are waiting till August to see what will happen ... God himself may not know.' Kumar says the company has been having meetings once a month.

Seated under a large blue-and-white Uninor umbrella outside a mobile phone shop in south Bangalore, 18-year-old Syyed exudes confidence. He says he sells at least 10–15 SIM cards a day. When asked if he was worried that Uninor might exit India, he says that will not happen. 'Bharosa hai [I have confidence], their licence will be renewed.'

The company has not told him anything about the possibility of shutting shop but neither have customers enquired about the issue, he says. Customers, he says, are attracted by Uninor's low tariffs. 'People buy up to four SIM cards a month because it is so cheap,' he says.

North Kolkata-based retailer Manoj Pandey, too, is not worried about his business suffering if Uninor shuts shop. The number of Uninor subscribers has gone up in Kolkata. Though employees at the Uninor office in Kolkata are concerned about losing their jobs, they say the fact that Brekke himself came down to the city and did a roadshow with them has reassured them.

Hundreds of miles away in Chennai, Karthik, a salesperson at a mobile retail shop, says Uninor officials have told him about the problems. 'Sales have come down since January-February. People ask for other connections even if we tell them about Uninor. We used to sell around 100 Uninor SIM cards a month. Now we don't sell even five a month,' he rues, adding that service standards too have dropped. 'The in-charge of this area is not showing interest and we hear he is looking for a job.'

Uninor, meanwhile, is continuing with its marketing initiatives, one of them being a tie-up with the producers of the recently released film Shanghai. For its target audience in Mumbai, Bangalore in Ahmedabad, the company has announced, 'Buy any Uninor connection and stand a chance to meet the star cast of Shanghai.'

As on date the courts have agreed for the auctioning of assets of Uninor and Telenor is likely to take over majority of the assets and is in look out for an alternative JV partner. However the process of repeat auction of the 2G spectrum is likely to go beyond the 31 August 2012 deadline given by the Supreme Court and the uncertainty continues.

Case Questions

1. Can Brekke and his men survive?

2. Is the HR strategy of using job security as a motivational tool sustainable in the present case?

3. Is it ethical to exploit 'uncertainty' in business of a competitor for poaching personnel and market share?

4. What is alternative business model you suggest for Telenor in India for sustenance and expansion in Telecom Industry?

SECTION II

CASE STUDIES IN FINANCE MANAGEMENT

Financial Accounting, Direct/Indirect Taxation, Banking and Insurance

5. An Elephantine Exercise
6. Wrong Signals for FDI Climate
7. One Nation One Tax
8. Economics, Markets, Public Life, and Regulators

5

An Elephantine Exercise

A Case Study on the Mergers of Major Banks in SBI

Learning Objectives

To analyse the financial implications of merging subsidiary entities with parent entity. To understand the complexities associated with personnel management in mergers. To estimate the possibility of 'too big to fail' syndrome creating a moral hazard.

Synopsis

State Bank of India seems to be biting off more than it can chew by merging five associate banks with itself. The merger with five associate banks (plus Bhartiya Mahila bank) will bring challenges for SBI in major districts in the country. More so, in states where the associate banks are headquartered—Rajasthan, Karnataka, Andhra Pradesh, Punjab, and Kerala. In fact, the branch gridlock is just one of the many pain points. For instance, the stressed loans of the five associate banks (gross NPAs and restructured loans) add up to a staggering Rs 35,396 crore. This amounts to almost half of SBI's stressed loans portfolio of Rs 66,117 crore in 2015/16. In contrast, the deposits, advances, and assets of these banks are less than one-fifth of SBI. The merger itself is the biggest in the Indian banking industry. The bank is swallowing five associate banks with assets of Rs 6.03 lakh crore—it's almost equal to the size of the country's largest private bank ICICI Bank that has assets of Rs 7.17 lakh crore. The merged SBI entity would have deposits of Rs 21 lakh crore; advances of Rs

Indian Business Case Studies. Priti Pachpande and Sham Bachhav, Oxford University Press. © ASM Group of Institutes, Pune, India 2022. DOI: 10.1093/oso/9780192869401.003.0005

18 lakh crore; net profits of Rs 11,589 crore; 24,000-plus branches; 58,000 ATMs and 270,000 employees. Compare these figures with ICICI Bank—deposits of Rs 4.21 lakh crore; advances of Rs 4.35 lakh crore; net profits of Rs 9,726 crore; 4,450 branches; 14,305 ATMs and 74,000 employees. 'It is easier to merge the balance sheet numbers, but the real challenge is to merge the people (and culture), products (and clients), branches (and personal touch), etc.,' remarks a banking consultant. This case study attempts to analyse the various implications, financial and others, of the merger of SBI with its five associate banks.

Is SBI Biting off More Than It Can Chew?

In the past decade, SBI managed to merge two associate banks. Many say the current decision to merge all the associate banks—State Bank of Travancore, Mysore, Hyderabad, Patiala, and Bikaner and Jaipur—is a bold decision. Motilal Oswal, a leading brokerage firm, in its report has observed that amalgamating all associate banks together and then merging that entity with SBI could have significantly reduced the integration risk. Is the government in some hurry? Even the government felt the need for continuity at this juncture by extending the term of Chairman Arundhati Bhattacharya for a year. A year ago, Bhattacharya herself had remarked that the time was not right to kick start the merger. 'There are a lot of challenges (that the bank is facing) and those challenges are more immediate than merging banks,' she had said. In a year, Bhattacharya has become a torchbearer for the government's push for consolidation. 'It's a win-win for both,' she says. Clearly, it's a forced merger by the owner (government), which is pushing for a mega consolidation to drive possible synergies. This merger is relatively easier as there is a holding company-subsidiary relationship. Bhattacharya is banking on the expanded reach. 'There will be efficiencies out of rationalisation of branches, a common treasury operation and proper deployment of a large skilled resource base,' says Bhattacharya. SBI's associate banks are a mirror image of the parent. The SBI chairman sits on their board. The product basket has many similarities with focus on infrastructure (especially power), iron and steel, textiles and other segments

like agriculture, home, and auto loans. Bhattacharya plans to spread
the branches out to get better reach. The bank has already kicked off
an exercise to use analytics to geographically locate each branch, find
out their profitability, footfalls, etc. It has already set in motion plans
to digitize the branches. 'Maybe some of it (excess) we will convert into
things like e-corner, branches that are more digitally powered with
lesser people. We have to look at a mix and match of all these things,'
says Bhattacharya.

Size Is the Only Driving Force

Mergers help in acquiring access to new geographies or product suite.
For instance, Kotak Mahindra Bank with 640-plus branches, mostly in
West and North India, acquired ING Vysya Bank for building a presence in a new geography. This Bangalore-headquartered bank had 570
branches, mostly in South India. The ING acquisition also brought
product expertise in crop loans, foreign exchange, and handling an
MNC client base. Similarly, HDFC Bank pounced on Centurion Bank
of Punjab for its presence in North India. In the SBI case, size is the
only targeted objective. 'Beyond a certain point, size doesn't matter to
help raise resources. SBI already enjoys a very good rating from global
agencies,' say experts. Globally, the merger will put the bank in the top
50, up from its current 52nd position. The other banks of the same
size globally are Canada's Bank of Montreal, Denmark's Danske Bank,
and Japan's Sumitomo Mitsui. But size is no longer a fad after the 2008
global financial meltdown, when the government had to use tax-payers'
money to bail out banks. Bernie Sanders, who recently failed to get the
Democratic nomination ahead of Hillary Clinton in the US presidential
election, has made a case for breaking up financial institutions too big
to fail. 'Half a dozen financial institutions hold assets equal to 60 per
cent of the GDP, 40 per cent of the bank deposits, more than two third
of the credit cards and 95 per cent of the derivative trades,' said Sanders.
SBI and ICICI Bank are already identified by the Reserve Bank of India
as systemically important banks (SIBs). But there is a huge difference
in their sizes—SBI will have a balance sheet of about Rs 30 lakh crore

post-merger against ICICI's Rs 7.7 lakh crore. SBI also has one-fifth of the share in the banking industry's deposits and advances. That clearly has the potential to create a systemic crisis. The risk stems from the fact that SBI is not in the top quartile in terms of performance. For instance, HDFC Bank, the second-largest private bank with one-fourth of the assets of SBI, has a market capitalization of Rs 3.26 lakh crore, far ahead of SBI's Rs 1.98 lakh crore.

Employee Anxieties

The rationalization of branches would be painful for both employees and customers. There is a fear amongst the associate banks' employees that their branches would be sacrificed in the bargain. 'Integration of 70,000 employees, which is 34 per cent of the parent workforce as against size of business of 25 per cent of the parent's, will be a key challenge,' says broking firm Motilal Oswal. Pradeep Shankar, former MD of State Bank of Indore, says new probationary officers at SBI get four increments at the time of confirmation. Officers of associate banks are not offered a similar deal, he points out. 'But there are fast-track promotions for officers in associate banks. The process is a bit slower in SBI because of its large size. These things have to be rationalised post-merger,' says Shankar. In the merged entity, seniority will matter more for further promotions than the designation. In the past, the retirement of a large number of people gave SBI a good opportunity to replace them with skilled people in technology, digital banking, advisory, treasury, etc. But the merger will not only put a lid on fresh recruitment but also force them to redeploy people from the excess workforce pool in new areas. However, Bhattacharya says the group is retiring about 13,000 people every year, which would neutralize the excess manpower. So, even if there is a little bit of extra staff, it would be adjusted in two years' time. 'I'm anyway set to lose 26,000 people in the next two years,' says Bhattacharya. Experts say managing a large organization like SBI would require organizational changes. A year after moving to the corner room, the SBI chief had actually sought two additional MD positions from the government apart from the current four MDs. 'We are still seeking those two positions,' says Bhattacharya.

A Laggard

SBI has higher cost, lower profits per employee, and lower return on assets than most private sector banks.

Banks	COST TO INCOME	OPERATING EXPENSES/ TOTAL INCOME	PROFIT PER EMPLOYEE	ROA (%)
SBI	0.49	28.12%	4.79	0.46
ICICI Bank	0.35	28.70%	14	1.49
HDFC Bank	0.44	34.23%	15	1.92
Axis Bank	0.38	29.49%	17.83	1.72
Kotak Bank	0.64	36.59%	7	1.19
Yes Bank	0.40	24.92%	20.96	1.78

Profit per employee in Rs lakh; Figures for 2015/16; Source: IBA

The Bad Bank

Over Rs 1 lakh crore of bad loans and still counting. This huge portfolio of NPAs is disconcerting. SBI will have to deploy huge resources—both capital and people—to resolve the problem. A major chunk of it is coming from the associate banks—almost half of it. Bhattacharya wants to take on the asset quality challenge head on. 'At the end of the day, associate banks are still part of my group company. Whatever they have is going to impact the group's balance sheet. It is better to understand what they are rather than ignore and hope that it would disappear,' she says. Many say the timing of the merger isn't right. SBI is swamped with bad assets, which requires provisioning from profits. Raising capital is a challenge because of low market valuations. Similarly, the disintermediation in financial services is taking place at a fast pace with new players like peer-to-peer (P2P) lenders, NBFCs, and tech-savvy private banks disrupting the payments landscape.

The challenges for the bank are far more significant than the merger. The danger is that the management bandwidth would be devoted to addressing the merger pangs. And even if the bank sails through the integration challenges, the consolidation won't deliver the results unless there are governance reforms, a culture of meritocracy, succession planning, and operational efficiencies. Until then, it's like 'An Elephant on the Prowl'.

The stress factor: SBI faces a tough year amidst sluggish loan growth, weak margins, and dodgy asset quality.

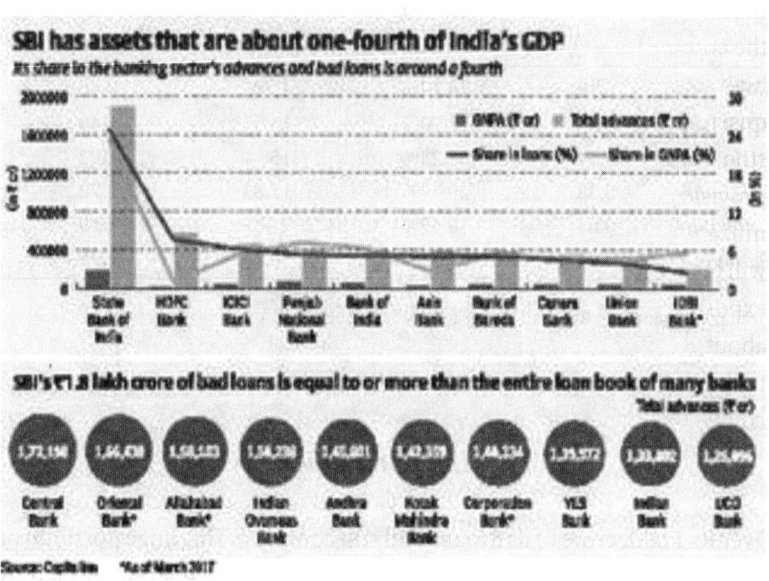

SBI has assets that are about one-fourth of India's GDP
Its share in the banking sector's advances and bad loans is around a fourth

SBI's ₹1.8 lakh crore of bad loans is equal to or more than the entire loan book of many banks

For SBI, India's largest bank that got bigger in April 2017 after merging its five associate banks, bad loans have grown in size too. While the consolidated picture on asset quality post-merger was expected to be a cause for concern, higher-than-expected slippages, has rankled investors. With gross non-performing assets at nearly a tenth of SBI's (merged entity) loans, the bank faces a tough year ahead amidst sluggish loan growth, weak margins, and dodgy asset quality. On standalone basis, SBI's GNPAs stood at 6.9% of loans as of March 2017 and that of its associates at 20%. The tally of GNPAs for the merged entity that stood at 9.1% in March has gone up to 9.97% of loans in June. Given that SBI accounts for about one-fourth of the total advances in the system, the size of its bad loans is worrisome for the sector as a whole. To put things in perspective, SBI's Rs. 1.8-lakh crore of bad loans as of June 2017, is now higher than the loan book of many banks. HDFC Bank, that ranks second, has a loan book which is just 30% of SBIs. The gap gets wider down the pecking order. Aside from SBI's huge stockpile of bad loans, slippages remain a cause for worry as well. Slippages for the merged entity for the June quarter stood at Rs. 26,249 crores, higher than the Rs. 25,000-odd crore in the previous quarter (Rs. 9,755 crores from SBI and the remaining from its associate banks). The pace of slippages from SBI's associate banks is likely to remain elevated and will continue to hurt the performance of the bank in the coming quarters. Even on standalone basis, SBI's slippages have been high at about Rs. 10,000 crores until the March 2017 quarter; three to four quarters prior to the asset quality review (AQR), SBI's quarterly slippages stood at Rs. 5,000–7,000 crore. Even if the pace of slippages is moderate, provisioning requirement for these bad loans are unlikely to come off significantly. This is because the ageing of bad loans (a large book at that) will lead to incrementally higher provisions in the coming quarters. SBI's exposure to the 12 accounts that are under the NCLT for resolution is about Rs. 50,247 crores. The management has stated that it will have to make an additional provisioning of Rs. 3,500 crores for FY18 on such accounts than what was factored in earlier.

Weak Core Performance

SBI's weak core performance also does not lend comfort. The bank's net interest income has declined by 3.5% year-on-year (y-o-y) in the June quarter. Loan growth (domestic) was a modest 1% during the quarter, far lower than the overall sector growth, which is already a meagre 5%. Private banks have managed to deliver far better growth. Even ICICI Bank and Axis Bank that have relatively higher exposure to stressed sectors delivered a higher 11–12% growth in loans in the June quarter. The retail segment for these banks continued to put up a strong show growing 18–22%. SBI's retail portfolio grew at a slower 13% in the June quarter. Elevated levels of stress in asset quality and sharp fall in its benchmark MCLR (60% of the loans are on MCLR) has kept net interest margin (NIM) for SBI under pressure. From 3% last year, NIM has fallen to 2.5% in the June quarter. Some of the pressure is also due to the bank's notable shift towards corporate bonds (from loans). Around Rs. 40,000 crores have moved from loans to corporate bonds over the past year. Given that the yields on loans are higher than that on bonds, it has impacted the bank's NIM to some extent. Further shift towards bonds, weak credit growth and pricing pressure are likely to keep margins under pressure. The management's guidance of 6–8% growth in loans for FY18, is more or less in line with the system growth, but lower than its earlier guidance of 11%. SBI's weak core performance and continuing pressure on asset quality are likely to weigh on the bank's earnings over the next year.

Conclusions

This merger would be a test case for a bigger consolidation among public sector banks (PSBs), which control more than two-thirds of the banking operations in India. Recently, Bank Board Bureau Chairman Vinod Rai hinted at a merger of two large PSBs in the near future. The government plans to have less than 10 large PSBs eventually, from 27 currently. 'We have seen this happening in China, Australia and Malaysia. In Australia, 80 per cent of banking is done by four large entities. The same is true for China. It does help if you have large organisations of similar size, right kind of governance framework, technology, etc.', says Bhattacharya.

Case Questions

1. Would an amalgamation of the associate banks and maintaining it as a separate entity have been better than the current merger?

2. What kind of reforms will be needed to make the new SBI as profitable as ICICI or HDFC?

3. Is the Indian financial system prepared to handle a 'Too big to fail' crisis in case of failure of the new SBI?

6

Wrong Signals for FDI Climate

A Case Study on Retrospective Taxation

Learning Objectives

The Securities and Exchange Board of India (SEBI) is the nodal office supposed to provide oversight in the compliance to tax provisions by all the Indian and foreign companies operating in India. The tax on certain financial transactions including the foreign company disposing of its assets to a third party without payment of the capital gain. Taxes have been observed to be countering the provisions of the tax on such transactions, and the central government has promulgated certain notifications which bring such revenues earned by foreign companies are liable to pay capital gains to the Indian government. And made the notification as retrospectively effective over the period when such a notification did not exist.

This is a major conflict between foreign investors in India who have established their operation in India.

This case study explains few of the anomalies which the foreign investors are very unhappy about and have filed petitions against tax authorities in courts outside India for adjudication. It is presently at a crucial face while tax agencies are demanding huge amounts as tax arrears and international courts have favoured the foreign companies petitions and asked for Indian tax authorities to set aside their tax claims.

Synopsis

Vodafone Group Plc is a British multinational telecommunications company headquartered in London and with its registered office in Newbury, Berkshire. It is the world's second-largest mobile telecommunications

Indian Business Case Studies. Priti Pachpande and Sham Bachhav, Oxford University Press. © ASM Group of Institutes, Pune, India 2022. DOI: 10.1093/oso/9780192869401.003.0006

company measured by both subscribers and 2013 revenues (in each case behind China Mobile), and had 434 million subscribers as of 31 March 2014. Vodafone owns and operates networks in 21 countries and has partner networks in over 40 additional countries. Its Vodafone Global Enterprise division provides telecommunications and IT services to corporate clients in over 65 countries.

Vodafone has a primary listing on the London Stock Exchange and is a constituent of the FTSE 100 Index. It had a market capitalization of approximately £89.1 billion as of 6 July 2012, the third-largest of any company listed on the London Stock Exchange. It has a secondary listing on NASDAQ.

Vodafone Essar Limited, formerly known as Hutchison Essar, is a telecom service provider in India that covers 23 telecom circles in India and is based in Mumbai.

Vodafone holds 67% stake in Vodafone Essar Limited and Essar holds the rest 33% stake.

On 11 February 2007, Vodafone agreed to acquire the controlling interest of 67% held by Li Ka Shing Holdings in Hutch-Essar for US$11.1 billion. The company was valued at USD 18.8 billion. The transaction closed on 8 May 2007. Despite the official name being Vodafone Essar, its products are simply branded 'Vodafone'. It offers both prepaid and postpaid GSM cellular phone coverage throughout India.

Operations Strategies

Vodafone Group has entered into arrangements with network operators in countries where the Group does not hold an equity stake. Under the terms of these Partner Market Agreements, Vodafone and its partner operators co-operate in the marketing of global products and services with varying levels of brand association. This strategy enables Vodafone to implement services in new territories and to create additional value to their partners' customers and to Vodafone's travelling customers without the need for equity investment in these countries.

Their diverse array of holdings ranges from some of the world's biggest port operators and retailers, to property development and infrastructure, to innovative and advanced telecommunications and data services.

Hutchison Whampoa

Hutchison Whampoa Limited (HWL) reported turnover of approximately HKD413 billion (USD53 billion) for the year ended 31 December 2013. Some of their achievements include being the world's leading port investor, developer, and operator, the world's leading health and beauty retailer and a pioneer of leading-edge mobile multimedia telecommunications.

With roots in Hong Kong in the 1800s, HWL's operations now span the globe. The multicultural mix of their executives and staff reflects the diversity and reach of their operations.

Essar

This is a multinational corporation with an annual turnover of US$39 billion and investments in steel, energy, information, and services. It employs more than 73,000 in about 25 countries.

Essar began as a construction company in 1969 and has diversified into manufacturing, services, and retail over the years since then. Over the last decade, it has grown through strategic global acquisitions and partnerships, capturing new markets and discovering new raw material sources.

Today, Essar continues to expand its global footprint, focusing on markets in Asia, Africa, Europe, the Americas, and Australia. Essar invests significantly in the latest technology to drive forward and backward integration in its businesses, and on leveraging synergies between these businesses. It also focuses on in-house research and innovation to be a low-cost manufacturer with high-quality products and innovative customer offerings.

Essar Global Fund (EGFL) is a diversified global investment fund with a diversified portfolio of investments across the sectors of energy, metals and mining, infrastructure, and services. The combined assets of Essar Power and Essar Oil constitute Essar Energy.

Hutchison Max Telecom Ltd (HMTL)

This is a joint venture between HWL and the Max Group, which was established on 21 February 1992. The license to operate in Mumbai (then Bombay) circle was awarded to Hutchison Max by the Department of Telecommunications (DoT) in November 1994. The cellular service branded 'Max Touch' was launched the same year switching and other related equipments were provided by Ericsson and the network was designed, engineered, and set up by Motorola. Hutchison Max entered into the Delhi telecom circle in December 1999, the Kolkata circle in July 2000, and the Gujarat circle in September 2000. Licenses for these circles had initially been awarded by the DoT in 1994, 1997, and 1995 respectively. Between 1992 and 2006, Hutchison acquired interests in all 23 mobile telecom circles of India.

Case Details

The case concerns a tax dispute between the Vodafone group and the Indian income tax (IT) authorities over the acquisition by Vodafone International Holdings BV (VIH) (part of the Vodafone group and a company resident for tax purposes in the Netherlands) of the entire share capital of CGP Investments (Holdings) Ltd (a company incorporated in Hong Kong but resident for tax purposes in the Cayman Islands) on 11 February 2007 for about $11 billion (Rs 55,000 crores) from Hutchison Telecommunications International Ltd (HTIL). CGP, through various intermediate companies/contractual arrangements, controlled 67% of Hutchison Essar Limited (HEL), an Indian company.

The acquisition resulted in Vodafone acquiring control over Hutch-Essar, a joint venture between the Hutchison group and the Essar group, which had obtained telecom licenses to provide cellular telephony in different circles in India in November 1994. Because the sale was supposed to have been made overseas, no taxes were paid in India.

The IT authorities in India contended that the primary aim of this transaction was to acquire 67% controlling interest in HEL, a company resident in India. They, therefore, sought to tax capital gains under Section 9(1)(i) of the Indian Income Tax Act 1961, (2) arising from the sale of the share capital of CGP on the basis that CGP, while not a tax resident in India, holds the underlying Indian asset.

According to the tax authorities the profit made by Hutchison Hong Kong, while it sold its shares of Hutch-Essar to Vodafone, was generated in India. Therefore, Vodafone, the buyer of the shares, had an obligation to withhold and pay the tax in India, before making the payment to Hutchison. The tax demand was $2.5 billion. Vodafone contested, stating that neither Vodafone nor Hutch was liable to pay the tax as both the companies were located outside India and the deal happened outside India.

Vodafone filed a writ petition in the Bombay High Court challenging the jurisdiction of the tax authorities. In September 2008 the Bombay High Court held that the transaction was one of transfer of capital assets situated in India, and accordingly, the Indian income tax authorities had jurisdiction over the matter. It concluded that it would be simplistic to assume that the entire transaction between HTIL and VIH was fulfilled merely upon the transfer of a single share of CGP in the Cayman Islands.

The two-judge bench noted that 'The commercial and business understanding between the parties postulated that what was being transferred from HTIL to VIH BV was the controlling interest in HEL ... HEL was at all times intended to be the target company and a transfer of the controlling interest in HEL was the purpose which was achieved by the transaction'.

The Supreme Court Verdict

The case went up to the Supreme Court and, based on two key but independent arguments, the highest court concluded that there was no merit in the High Court's verdict. The first line of reasoning was that the transaction between Vodafone and Hutch was a share transfer (sale) rather than a transfer of capital assets and that the ownership of the capital assets remained vested in the Indian company.

The judgment took recourse to the legal distinction between a company and its shareholders and thus the judgment does not make a distinction between shareholding that constituted a controlling interest and that which was a pure financial investment. Consequently it becomes completely immaterial in this specific case that the share(s) actually transferred were not of the company located in India but of offshore companies that ultimately controlled the shares that constituted the controlling interest in the Indian company. Even if the shares were of a company located in India, in the court's view it would not have constituted a transfer of capital assets.

Once it is accepted that the shareholders of a company have a legal identity distinct from the company, no matter what the proportion of shares they hold, it follows that the two companies would have distinct identities even if one held a controlling share in the other. The Supreme Court judgment makes it a point to emphasize that even a subsidiary has an identity that is distinct from its parent holding company.

The second interesting aspect of the Supreme Court judgment is that it argues for a 'look at' test in which tax authorities consider the entire Hutchison structure as it existed, 'holistically', at its face value, and not adopt a 'dissecting approach'. In other words, authorities should not ask whether the transaction is a tax avoidance method, but apply the 'look at' test to ascertain its legal nature.

The Supreme Court was not in favour of the High Court's 'look through' test because, it claimed, this was inconsistent with the need for certainty and consistency of tax policies that are crucial for taxpayers' confidence (especially foreign investors). The judgment argues that such a going behind the 'corporate veil' or looking through would be legitimate only in cases where it can be established that there is a deliberate intention of evading taxes.

In the Supreme Court's view no such inference can be made in this case if the steps that led to the creation of the complex holding structure of Vodafone and the eventual Vodafone-Hutch transaction were seen in the proper context. According to the court the structuring of the transfer of control from Hutch to Vodafone was not done with the specific intention of avoiding taxes. Hence the corporate veil need not be pierced and the fact that there was a transfer of control from Hutch to Vodafone must be ignored. And thus the tax authorities should concern themselves only with the corporate structure of a merger deal, and not of what assets are changing hands. The court also felt as Vodafone is doing business in India for a long-time intention of avoiding capital gains tax is not visible.

The Underlying Issues Involved

Why 'look at' and not 'look through'?

The first interesting issue that arises is why authorities should (a) look at and (b) not look through the transactions, especially if what is being examined are complex transactions of mammoth corporations like Vodafone? After all, even simple cases of wrongdoing may not be caught out without looking at the substance of the act beyond the mere form of what is being claimed by the parties.

Cayman Islands are a small area and it is famous for notorious activities and safe area for pirates and deserters in yesteryears. Transactions in these areas should normally be viewed with suspicion that has not been taken into consideration in the case.

Amendment which Created the Issue

Key budget provisions affecting mergers and acquisition and corporate restructuring.

The Finance Bill, 2012 ('Bill' or 'Budget') is out and has attracted a lot of attention especially to the enforcement provisions and the retrospective amendments. An attempt has been made in this note to identify, compile, and comment on provisions which are likely to have an effect on mergers and acquisitions and corporate restructuring exercises post-enactment of this Bill.

1. A retrospective change taxing indirect transfer of shares of an Indian Company. Clause 47 (iv)

Section 9 of the Income Tax provides cases of income, which are deemed to accrue or arise in India. This is a legal fiction created to tax income, which may or may not arise in India and would not have been taxable but for the deeming provision created by this section. Sub-section (1) (i) provides a set of circumstances in which income accruing or arising, directly or indirectly, is taxable in India.

One of the limbs of clause (i) is income accruing or arising directly or indirectly through the transfer of a capital asset situated in India. The legislative intent of this clause through this budgetary amendment is to widen the application as it covers incomes, which are accruing or arising directly or indirectly out of the assets/investments in India to the person resident outside India. The section codifies source rule of taxation wherein the state, where the actual economic nexus of income is situated has a right to tax the income irrespective of the place of residence of the entity deriving the income.

Where corporate structure is created to route funds, the actual gain or income arises only in consequence of the investment made in the activity to which such gains are attributable and not the mode through which such gains are realized. Thus the source country has taxation right on the gains derived from offshore transactions where the value is attributable to the underlying assets.

Current Position

Vodafone Group has already begun an international arbitration against the Indian government in more than Rs. 20,000 crores tax case. The Indian government has appointed former Chief Justice of India RC Lahoti as arbitrator in the tax dispute.

The arbitration stems from a tax dispute over Vodafone's acquisition of Hutchison Whampoa's Indian assets in 2007. The government has maintained that the transaction is taxable because it involves Indian assets. Vodafone says Indian tax laws don't apply as the transaction occurred between two overseas companies.

In 2012, the Supreme Court ruled that Vodafone was not liable to pay taxes on its acquisition. Later that year, the government changed rules to enable it to tax deals that had already been concluded.

The government's initial tax demand of Rs. 7,990 crores in 2007 has now risen to nearly Rs. 20,000 crores because of interests and penalty.

Uncertainties over tax policy in India have unsettled investors, and tax claims on foreign companies have been a major concern. IBM Corp, Royal Dutch Shell Plc, and Nokia are among foreign firms contesting local tax claims.

In the context of the above and present need for improving investors climate in the country can the government do away with certain laws or has Vodafone taken the matter too far is the question which comes to the mind of a common citizen. So the following questions can help to clear the air in this regard.

Case Questions

1. How is the case of taxation of the accrued interest on two foreign organizations completing an acquisition deal of their assets in a third country is looked in to by international courts?

2. Why is Vodafone not exiting from Indian market in spite of huge alleged tax liabilities? Do they feel that they have a weaker case? Why did they offer to make an out of court settlement of the claimed tax dues from IT?

3. What is likely to be a global investments impact for fresh FII or FDI in India in view of the above case? What are the likely consequences if the case settled either way? What according to you would be a win-win resolution for both the parties involved?

7

One Nation One Tax

A Case Study on Goods and Services Tax (GST) India

Learning Objectives

What is the GST bill? What does it mean to you and me?

The Good and Services Tax is the biggest indirect tax reform since 1947 and it has potential to lead the economic integration of India. This will be levied on manufacture sale and consumption of goods and services.

In the words of the finance minister, the GST bill will lead to the economic integration of India.

The main function of the GST is to transform India into a uniform market by breaking the current fiscal barrier between states. Thus the GST will facilitate a uniform tax levied on goods and services across the country.

Currently, the indirect tax system in India is complicated with overlapping taxes levied by the Centre and the State separately.

Framework of the GST will replace indirect taxes.

The GST will have a 'dual' structure, which means it will have two components—the Central GST and the State GST. They will both have separate powers to legislate and administer their respective taxes. Thus equally empowering both.

Taxes such as excise duty, service, central sales tax, VAT (value added tax), entry tax, or octroi will all be subsumed by the GST under a single umbrella.

With passing of the GST bill, we can expect a climate of improved tax compliance.

Thus, the GST will basically have only three kinds of taxes, Central, State, and another called the integrated GST to tackle inter-state transactions.

Indian Business Case Studies. Priti Pachpande and Sham Bachhav, Oxford University Press. © ASM Group of Institutes, Pune, India 2022. DOI: 10.1093/oso/9780192869401.003.0007

When is the proposed GST set to start functioning and what are the hurdles?

The GST regime is intended to be functional from 1 April 2016.

The main concerns over the bill—1% additional tax as goods move across states, the constitutional cap of 18%, and an independent dispute redressed mechanism.

The Impact and Relevance of the GST Bill

According to Finance Minister the GST will be instrumental in helping the GDP of India to grow by 2%.

The GST also offers a solution to the multinationals as it breaks down the indirect tax structure into one single tax payable by the companies.

Although the states have feared loss of fiscal powers, the Constitutional amendment bill has promised to solve this by giving compensation packages for three years for any kind of revenue loss.

The bill has proposed to have GST council wherein all union and state ministers in charge of finance will be on an equal footing. It will also have a dispute settlement authority to mitigate the tensions between the centre and state smoothly.

One main contention for the state in the GST is the inclusion of petroleum products. The current consensus on this is that the states will continue to levy sales tax/VAT on these with the exception of imports and inter-state trade.

Agarwal Packers and Movers Ltd., one of the largest logistics companies in India, evolved from a small-scale business of Agarwal Household Carrier established in 1987 and functioned particularly for the shifting of household goods. Incepted by vision and hard efforts of Shri Ramesh Agarwal and Shri Rajender Agarwal, the company moved ahead towards the path of growth.

This evolution takes place on the solid grounds of expansion in terms of proficient and customer-satisfactory services. It is a logistic subsidiary of Agarwal Household Carrier established in 1987 and functioned particularly for the shifting of household goods. Agarwal movers group is a business conglomerate having its reach in Aviation Logistics, Packing and moving (both National and International), Transportation, Warehousing, 3PL, Cube-on-line Freight station, and other related activities.

Mr Ramesh Agarwal is the founder of Agarwal Packers and Movers and he played an important role in keys areas of development of transport and logistics. The company employs 2,900 plus employees. The company maintains secure warehouse facilities for smoother transition of goods from one place to another. They believe in zero trans-shipment, i.e., shifting of loads from one vehicle to another. They have 'trucking cube concept' which allows the customer to share the carrier instead of booking the whole of it thereby saving cost and company saving its fuel. Agarwal Packers is an entrusted brand and has been able to serve more than 14 lacs of household till date and have registered themselves in 'Limca book of records' for being the 'Largest mover of household goods' for the years 2013 and 2014.

The company is one of the major members of IAM (International Association of Movers), USA. The company aim to meet global standards to compete in dynamically expanding industries. They have international presence across 182 countries and have their patent/TM registered in countries like Canada, USA, Australia, etc. It has its corporate offices spread across major Indian cities like Delhi, Hyderabad, and Kolkata. They are planning to raise funds to acquire supply chain companies and expand their relocation services.

Current Issues

The indirect tax regime in India is not only complex (with multiple taxes applicable on a business) but also widely seen to be inefficient and opaque. One of the features of the current system is that taxes are non-creditable either due to restrictions in the law or because there is no comparison between central and state levies. Furthermore, as a result of multiple applicable levies, an assessee engaged in the manufacture of goods, sale of goods, and provision of services has to comply with payment, reporting, and audit requirements under different tax authorities.

Challenges Currently Faced by the Logistic Industry in India

Logistics cost in India is about 13–14% of the GDP, as against 7–8% in developed countries. The sector faces multiple challenges due to poor conditions of storage infrastructure, inefficiencies in transportation, poor roads, a complex tax structure, and low rate of technology adoption. Pending issues with GST is also hampering growth.

The sector, as a whole, is not very organized and the work is competitive, especially in the big cities, where there are a vast number of unorganized small truck owners and service providers providing stiff competition at razor-thin margins. Technology adoption in the sector is also very low which is leading to lower efficiency and unlike European countries.

Overloading of trucks is the cause of enormous rate of death since logistics service providers do not consider investing in security measures due to cost reasons. The sector also faces storage and warehouse related risks as the fragmented private logistics companies do not interface with logistic chains.

The sector is also in need of skilled manpower as truck drivers face difficulty in accurately logging delivery records, understanding delivery documents, negotiating for return business, handling queries, and so on.

Logistics business operates on wafer-thin margin because of cut-throat competition in the sector with most of the operators with small fleet of vehicles. A cut in tax deducted at source (TDS) will help the industry immensely.

Limitations

Grey areas in service tax ruling results in unnecessary harassment and these need to be sorted out in the budget, Mr Agarwal said adding early implementation of GST will help the industry. The industry loses Rs 18,000 crore business because of delay at toll gates and this will get eliminated with rollout of GST.

'To make things more structural, formation of a regulatory logistic body by uniting key policy stakeholders across ministries for any integrated approach towards project planning and development is required,' he said.

GST: A New Road for Transportation and Logistics Industry in India

Currently, each of India's 29 states taxes goods that move across their borders at different rates and, as a result, freight that moves across the country is taxed multiple times. India is all set to usher in a game-changing tax reform—GST. Apart from creating a unified market across India, GST will help make India's manufacturing competitive by cutting high logistics and warehousing costs.

The regulatory reforms proposed in the GST presents a golden opportunity to revisit, rationalize, and re-engineer transportation and logistics networks, given the inherent inefficiencies with taxes based on the crossing of administrative boundaries or border checkpoints. Taxation at a national level, rather than by each state, will result in more efficient cross-state transportation, streamlining paperwork for road transporters and bringing down logistics costs.

The planned GST system seeks to replace around 15 state and federal taxes and tariffs for a single tax at the point of sale. The prevailing complicated tax structure in India meant that logistics decisions, including the choice of setting up inventory and distribution centres, are taken based on the tax regime such as central sales tax and state value-added tax (VAT) rates, rather than on operational efficiency. Tax optimization and administration is often considered over the operational and logistics efficiency.

GST will unleash a new era of developing logistics infrastructure and take investments to the next level. Given that the inefficient and longer supply chains with warehouses in almost every state is fiscally preferred in the existing regime, it is now time to overhaul and compress the entire logistics set-up. Last few months back, the Indian cabinet approved for introduction in Parliament a constitutional amendment bill to implement the much-awaited GST that seeks to unify India into a common market by replacing levies imposed by states and the centre.

Case Questions

1. How will the GST impact the logistics Industry?

2. According to you will the freight charges be adversely or positively impacted?

3. Do you feel whether in the long run the One Nation one Tax (GST) will benefit the Indian business?

8

Economics, Markets, Public Life, and Regulators

A Case Study on Global Economics

Learning Objectives

Indian Government over the previous few years has promulgated several ordinances and Acts for the implementation of Reforms in the Economic and Financial Aspects (fiscal reforms). However there is no clear analysis and notification regarding the impact of such reforms will have on the overall economic, financial social, and regulatory provisions. There is therefore a confused situation while implementing the reforms. This case studies throw some light on such conflict situation as seen through the narratives of many global economic and financial experts.

Synopsis

Newspapers reported PM's ideas on India's future development design by building on economic success and lifting vast sections of people out of poverty, at second Airtel Economic Times Global Business Summit GBS held in Delhi on 29 January 2014. PM claimed having achieved a great deal since his government took over in May 2014.

The summit was attended by GSK CEO Andrew Witty, GE VC John Rice, McKinsey MD Dominic Barton, Bharti Enterprises Chairman Mr Sunil Mittal, Aditya Birla Group Chairman Kumar Manglam Birla, Vedanta Chairman Mr Anil Agarwal and Adani Group Chairman Mr Gautam Adani. The government is seeking to boost economy through

Indian Business Case Studies. Priti Pachpande and Sham Bachhav, Oxford University Press. © ASM Group of Institutes, Pune, India 2022. DOI: 10.1093/oso/9780192869401.003.0008

Make in India by improving ease of doing business and driving invest-ments, mainly foreign.

India's infrastructure spending in 2011 was 8% ($ 112 billion) of country's GDP that was $ 1.4 trillion. Pradeep Singh MD of IDFC Project LTD opines that India must spend 10% of GDP on infrastructure to achieve and sustain economic growth target of 9% in coming years. $ 1 trillion are envisaged to be invested in infrastructure between 2012 and 2017. IMF has estimated India's GDP growth at 7.3% and Global GDP at 3.4% for 2015–16. With Rs 105.52 lakh crore GDP it shows 7.2% growth in 2014–2015 fiscal. India contributed 7.4% of Global GDP in purchasing power terms in 2014–2015 but its contribution in global growth is higher at 12.5%. Finance Minister Mr Arun Jaitley thinks 'India can achieve 8% growth in GDP in 2015–16 and that 7–7.5% growth is below poten-tial', he said at Suresh Neotia Memorial Lecture of CII at Kolkata on 29 January 2016.

VC of DE, John Rice at Global Business Summit (GBS), stated that plenty of capital was waiting to be invested in the country (India). However he put a rider by saying, 'The benchmarks are global. So when we think about the cost of doing business, we have to compare ourselves with the best country out there.'

Almost at the same time delivering CD Deshmukh Memorial lecture in New Delhi on 29 January 2016, Raguram Rajan, Governor of Reserve Bank of India warned against generating economic growth through additional debt saying that any deviation from the fiscal consolidation path will hurt stability of the economy; and that the government and RBI should continue to bring down inflation. He reinforces his view by saying, 'As Brazil's experience suggests, the enormous cost of becoming an unstable country far outweigh any small growth benefits that can be obtained through aggressive policies'. He also mentioned that fiscal def-icit of the Centre and State rose to 7.2% in 2014–2015 from 7% in pre-vious year.

Fortunately oil prices have fallen dramatically by 50% in the last one year (from January to December 2015) and this has helped a lot in re-ducing India's import bill and saving forex. Total merchandise exports are down nearly 18% in April–December 2015 period. The current ac-count deficit (CAD) is expected to be around 1.3% of GDP in fiscal 2015–2016. The news states that unsponsored American Depository Receipts

(ADRs) and Global Depository Receipts (GDRs) are likely to get capital gain tax relief in union budget 2016–17. Current law exempts ADRs and GDRs if they are backed by listed Indian stocks. On the same day *The Indian Express* captions news 'Government plans to defuse ticking bank bombs' meaning bad loan or NPAs of around Rs. 3 lakh crore's or 4.6% of advances by March 2015 are casting shadow on the ability of banks to lend. PMO and Finance Minister are discussing ways to operationalize an Asset Reconstruction Company (ARC) with help of IMF. It is estimated that total stressed assets of banks are not less than 7 lakh crore rupees. *The Indian Express* of 8 February 2016 reports that bad debts of Rs. 1.14 lakh crores were written off by state-owned banks, between 2013 and 2015, more than done in preceding nine years.

RBI Governor Mr Raghuram Rajan has for long resisted bringing interest rates down, in spite of government pressure. He has spoken on issues of serious nature such as in a V. Kurien Memorial lecture at IRMA Anand on 25 November 2014 he said 'We need a change in mindset where a willful defaulter is not lionized as a caption of industry, but justly chastised as a freeloader on the hardworking people of this country'.

From the perspective of a businessman, profit is the main objective of all the activities. And profit is positive difference between income or revenue and expenses or costs. Thus for maximizing profit the business has to either increase revenue side continually or lower the expense side on all occasions.

A business takes industry risk meaning level and volatility in earnings dependent on demand, extent of competition, bargaining power of suppliers, and economic factors. Then there is financial risk for a business wherein it has to live in a balancing exercise of paying shareholders, creditors, employees, and governments. Pressure of market will be translated in terms of net receivables. When we look at the revenues actually we are looking at what is happening with our customers. If customers are doing well then our business will do well as well.

Michael Sandel a Philosopher from Harvard University puts a question as, 'The years leading to financial crisis of 2008 were a heady time of market faith and deregulation—an era of market triumphalism'. The era began in easily 1980s when Ronald Regan and Margaret Thatcher proclaimed their conviction that markets, not government, held the key to prosperity and freedom. And it continued in 1990s with market-friendly liberalism of Bill Clinton and Tony Blair, who moderated but consolidated the faith that market is the primary mean for achieving the public good.

Today that faith is in doubt. The era of market triumphalism has come to an end. The financial crisis did more than cast doubt on the ability of markets to allocate risk efficiently. It also prompted a widespread sense that markets have become detached from morals. Most economists prefer not to deal with moral questions at least not in their role as economists.

They say their job is to explain people's behaviour, not judge it. But despite their protection, economists increasingly find themselves entangled in moral question. In the past economists dealt with avowedly economic topics—inflation and unemployment, savings and investments, interest rates and foreign trade. They explained how countries become wealthy and how the price system aligns with supply and demand for goods. Recently, however, many economists offer, they argue, 'It is not merely a set of insights about a production and consumption of material goods but also a science of human behavior.'

Raghuram Rajan does not mince words. He speaks his mind again at Nani Palkhivala Memorial lecture 'Strengthening Free Enterprise' on 4 February 2016 in Mumbai by saying 'Multinational Corporations complain all the time about excessive taxation but it is also true that Multinational Corporations across the world tend to find tax avoidance and sometimes tax evasion as appropriate techniques.

Some corporations find that all their intellectual property is manufactured in Cayman Island. I haven't seen lot of smart scientists sitting in Cayman Islands.' He was criticizing in the backdrop of firms such as Vodafone and Shell. In fact tax avoidance by companies such as Google, Apple, and scores of global firms have led to new laws across the world.

Case Question

1. What is your opinion on the long term effects of the economic reforms initiated by the government?

SECTION III

CASE STUDIES IN MULTIDISCIPLINARY AREAS MARKETING, STRATEGY, OPERATIONS

*Marketing Management, Strategic Management
Mergers and Acquisitions, and Operations Strategy*

9. The Candy Lounge
10. From Rags to Riches
11. Racing to Deliver
12. The Wings on Fire
13. A Good Strategy for Growth?
14. Transformative Turnaround Strategy
15. 'One' versus 'Many'
16. E-mobility—From the Current to the Future
17. What Really Went Wrong with Snapdeal?
18. The BSNL Saga
19. Future of the 'Future Group'
20. ITC at Cross Roads

9

The Candy Lounge

A Live Case Study on a Mexican Industry on Entrepreneurship

Learning Objectives

The major objective of this live case study is mainly to improve the manufacturing and sales of candies through Kiosk Stores in Mexico. This case study highlights a business venture to increase the sales in a profitable manner with sustainability. With change the method of promotion with a kiosk thus connecting the customer directly. Here we can also find the concepts used for cost and product pricing strategy.

Synopsis

The Candy Lounge is about an entrepreneurial business venture started and owned by Dr Jorge Palacio, an astute businessman from Ensenada, Baja California in western Mexico. It is a highly promising and prospering business in the manufacture and sale of Candies and other confectionary items through a Kiosk type stores in Ensenada and other places in Mexico. The proprietor entrepreneur is highly knowledgeable, ambitious, and motivated to excel in this venture by providing the best of products and services to the current and prospective markets. The owner has a keen sense of the competition as also the customer preferences and has taken adequate steps to ensure the best of customer relations and loyalty. While he is aware of the growing market demands of candy and related confectionery items as also the speed at which he needs to expedite investment decisions for aggressive marketing strategy, he is handicapped by inadequate cash flow and fresh investments for modernization of

Indian Business Case Studies. Priti Pachpande and Sham Bachhav, Oxford University Press. © ASM Group of Institutes, Pune, India 2022. DOI: 10.1093/oso/9780192869401.003.0009

manufacturing process along with tackling vendor-related issues. The enterprise has to break out of these barriers to meet its business objectives and targets come what may.

The Case Details

M/S Batilongo Candy lounge, a small-scale business enterprise for the manufacture and direct supplies to the consumers of Candies in different varieties and configurations along with all its accompaniments was established in 2011 by Dr Jorge Palacio & Family—in Ensenada a port city in Mexico about 100kms from Tijuana a major industrial hub in Baja California. The initial investments in plant and machinery including stores were of the order of $65,000.00 and most of it was met through family savings. (The working capital needs are met through revenues from the same business.) The installed plant capacity is to process 100 litres of tamarind pulp and to convert the same into Candies in different configurations and tastes to about 240–250 delivery to customers through its stores.

The unit is currently being managed by two senior members from the Palacio family (the managing director and the operations director) supported by 8–10 workmen at the shop and store levels. The business is managed through two Candy Stores in Ensenada and one point of sale in Tijuana as also online sales through companies website and payments through PayPal. Within a span of 2–3 years the company has registered annual revenues of $540,000.00 at an EBITDA of 18%

Vision: 'To provide our customers always with a comfortable ambience at store level sit outs and lounges, where they can enjoy & satisfy their cravings for delicious candies as per their taste, desires & status. We will excel in our Service & product Quality at competitive prices (Value for Money)'

Mission: 'To become a bench mark for comparison of product and service quality in the Candy Lounge business in the entire Mexico.'

Organizational Objectives (5–10 Years Plan)

1. To open **50 stores** in the next five years in entire country—Mexico.
2. To achieve in the next five years **2nd best level** performer status amongst all candy lounge stores in Mexico.
3. Launch an aggressive export strategy by establishing company-owned stores in USA and focus on improving exports necessary for growth and expansion of business.

The Chosen Business Strategy

1. To establish and sustain competitive advantage status in product and service quality over the nearest competitor.
2. To adopt the best cost strategy comparable with competition for product pricing.
3. Leverage business growth strategy through investments in strategic alliances and partnerships for meeting service and product quality standards not only at par but exceeding our nearest competitor.

Market Scenario: Major Competitors

1. Lucas, Pulparindo, Hola—for candy
2. Chilim Balam—for Candy Lounge3. OXXO, Costoco, Soriana, Commercial Mexicana—Retail major customers for candy stores are direct consumers mostly female in the age group of 13–22 years.

Operational Details over Previous Year
2011–2012

1. Fixed assets—$55000.00
2. Current assets—$ 55000.00 (in case of Batilongo FA & CA are same)
3. Current liabilities—$12000.00
4. Gross working capital—$6000.00

5. Gross revenue—$350,000.00
6. Gross margin—45%
7. Interest cost—7%
8. Taxes and tariffs—11%
9. Gross depreciation—20%
10. Net profit—$170,000.00 (rounded to nearest 100)

New Projects Needing Fresh Investments

1. Finishing and entertainment equipment for stores: $12,000.00
2. High volume packaging machine: $13000.00
   (The company has no ready cash for these investments)
3. For opening new stores: $ 30,000.00 per store
4. For new processing equipment: $10,000.00

Note: There is no financial issue for the working capital for current operations. Precautions are required for investments for expansion/growth since the market for Candy products is seasonal with lower sales in October–January. The financial resources for growth projects have limitations.

General Information on Batilongo Candy Stores

Organization set up is basically closely held family-managed enterprise, the directors are the owners and look into the financial aspects of the company personally. Besides the overall operations management including manufacture and marketing are also under the direct control of the directors. The operational requirements of lean manufacturing and 5s implementation, etc. are left to senior operative supervisors.

The wage and salary levels at Batilongo are comparable to industry standards (9–10%) excluding directors remunerations and commissions. The employee relations so far have been highly cordial and there is no labour union. The owners take care of orientation and appraisals of employees and also are aware of normal industry labour turnover of around 20% pa.

Major Vendor Base (Supply Chain)

There are in total 10 major suppliers of raw material and packaging material with a gross procurement of $ 125,000.00 PA (Annual Purchases are 36% of the manufacturing cost) with a provision for $3000.00 raw material and finished goods inventory. The company uses its own Logistics for inbound material for outward it depends on various courier and transport facilities. They use in house developed POS (Point of Sale) ERP system for inventory and reorder levels. Have standardized BOM for vendor base consolidation and negotiations. The usual supply chain issues are short supplies of key component the tamarind pulp and few more components. The company has made alternate arrangements to avoid production bottlenecks.

Manufacturing Strategy

Process Choice

1. For Pulp—continuous process @ 180 litters per day
2. For Candy-Batch type production—Make to stock
3. For store level operations—on-demand, make to order.

Process technology and productivity: Normal manually operated blenders, use of pull system for production. Candy productivity is at 70% of industry average, whereas store-level productivity is 120.0% of industry average. Kaizen techniques are under implementation at Candy manufacture. At candy store 80.0% of dishes are produced in less than 45 seconds an industry bench mark.

Process quality: FPY 99.0%—2% rejection at store level.

Modernization Plans and Projects

The organization is busy generating its own resources for the purchase of semi-automatic filler machine for candy processing high volume automatic sachet type packaging machine for candy processing.

Three smoothie machines for store operations.

Projects: New business model for 'Franchise' operations is ready is under negotiations with domestic parties. For establishing retail stores in domestic and US markets the market survey is underway.

Organizational Capability (Strategic Advantage) Profile

Finance: As of today finance is neither a core strength nor a distinctive competence.

Technology: Is a core strength but not a distinctive competence.

Human Resources: Is a core strength as also a distinctive competence.

Value chain management is a core strength as also a distinctive competence.

Opportunities to suit organizational capability: In Mexico small candy manufacturers, such as Lucas and others once they are well known have been taken over by much larger companies (Pepsico) offering maximum returns. Such a possibility exists for Batilongo once they are established in the marketplace. The current focus however is to develop franchise systems on priority. The organization is planning to avail small-term subsidized loans ($6 to 9k) from the government schemes for its future projects. The organization does not contemplate any immediate diversification plans till such time they have increased the number of candy lounges as per its set objectives.

There are plenty of opportunities in improving the operational technology. The organization is scouting for its requirement of new design packaging machines this would be of great help in expanding the candy business, besides support early to market for new products constantly developed by in house R&D.

The management is also keenly in lookout for the governments new incentive schemes for small businesses which would help in new investments for automated food processing machines and help rationalize operational costs.

Likely Threats in Future for Batilongo
Candy Lounge

Financial: The constant increase in the costs of raw materials (@4–6% pa) has to be absorbed by the business which reduces the margins which can only be neutralized by improving operational efficiencies or looking for alternate suppliers, which again is not a long-term measure. In respect of funds for future projects of expansion the company is not comfortable financially.

Technical: The market is flooded with new products from competition at frequent intervals which needs constant vigil and market intelligence surveys for which a planned marketing cell is not presently in place. The organization therefore is not in full knowledge of surprise moves by competition for introduction of new products and new marketing strategies

Human Resources: The threat of poaching skilled technicians between competition is rampant, even though skill building is not a difficult issue rebuilding the team creates hurdles in operational efficiency.

From the Horse's Mouth

This is what the owner director of Batilongo Candy Lounge has to say about his business: We found a different business model for traditional Candy and dish. We have been successful in introducing this concept in to the market. We have opened two permanent stores and one mobile (truck mounted) is now popular in the market. We have received more than 25,000 likes on our Facebook page for this new concept. Every one of our packaged products has its own identity in terms of cart on character and distinct packaging.

Our candy lounges provide nice sit-outs with surround music and Wi-fi connectivity and decorated layouts. Our innovatively prepared dishes, excellent quality, and unique service standards make the Candy Lounges a preferred 'Place to Be-in' the city. We serve around 250–310 people per day for 362 days in a year basic. But we are plagued by the high employee turnover in spite of attractive salary levels.

We definitely need to develop a new employee retention policy and practices. We also are worried about the funds required for our expansion plans including up-gradation of our stores' facilities. We are not very clear (do not have a business model) about our franchise business plans, our distribution and marketing capabilities are not adequate for national-level competition and expansions in our business.

Our future worries are on the severe competition we have to face at the national level with giants such as Pepsico and others (like sharks in the mid-sea). Even we need to prepare for such competition becoming severe at our doorsteps in Ensenada. (The cost of opening a new candy lounge is around $30–35k including all equipment POS system Electronic Cash Registers, Furniture and fixtures, all signages, three weeks inventory of consumables, we do not see any profits with this level of investment costs the additional cost of franchise will be 5% of gross sales plus 2% of shared margins for marketing expenses.

We also need to provide 5 hours of remote connectivity and 3 hours of onsite support for the franchise operations. Besides we need to train and ensure that the franchise does not resort to any shortcuts in adhering to our established quality and service standards.)

Conclusions

The Batilano Candy Lounge is about an entrepreneurial business venture. It is a highly promising and prospering business. It aimed to bring the best products and services to the current and prospective market. This continually strives to keep itself at the forefront of the product quality and customer retention Batilano Candy company has positioned itself strategically to increase its brand value and create a niche market for its products.

According to their chosen strategy to enhance competitive advantage in product over the nearest competition. Pricing is a major factor that affects customers buying instincts. To overcome the pricing challenge they introduced the kiosk concept for creating uniqueness in the sales. Their main concern is to find more methods of expansion plans, including the franchise options.

Case Questions

1. It is like 'Small is Beautiful' paradise for present level of business for Batilongo Candy Lounge. Even though there is enough confidence in managing present business. There could major hick-ups as the business has to expand and be ready for severe market forces.

2. What could be a robust business model which while accounting for current core and distinctive competencies of the organization would navigate the enterprise to expand and achieve its set objectives in line with its organizational vision and long-term mission?

3. Do you think that the present management is overconfident of its capabilities due to the success sclerosis so far? What will happen in future eventualities of succession plans and generation gaps when perhaps the very approach to business may need re-visioning and re-strategizing? Do you think the mission statement of the current set-up is inclusive of such radical restructuring need in future?

10

From Rags to Riches

A Case Study Mexion Wheels Private Limited India

Learning Objectives

To understand the impact of cost on the profitability of an organization. To understand the importance of a sound materials management policy and strategy in an organization. To understand the importance inter-departmental communication and coordination.

Synopsis

The lack of micro-management and absence of cost management focus normally leads to long-term drain on profit margins and business loss. Sometimes more than required efforts in managing cost and avoidance of waste may lead to improved sustainability even during overall depressive scenario at marketplace. The case highlights the importance of having sound materials management policy in an organization and also the need for communication within different department dealing with similar issues and problems. The case study deals with the negative effects of mismanagement of business processes including scrap generation and disposal.

Background of the Company

Mexion Wheels is a multi-national company specializing in manufacturing of wheel rims for various automobiles including a range of products such as trucks, bus, passenger cars, and small cars. The company's product

Indian Business Case Studies. Priti Pachpande and Sham Bachhav, Oxford University Press. © ASM Group of Institutes, Pune, India 2022. DOI: 10.1093/oso/9780192869401.003.0010

portfolio includes 40 different products and its customer portfolio includes 20 automotive manufacturing companies. Volume of production varies from 80,000 wheels to 1, 20,000 wheels per month.

Growth Story

The company was started in 1995. The main objective of the promoters was to use the idle land available and start a low technology auto component product. Company started manufacturing of wheel rims for Tata Motors and slowly increased its capacity to match the production demand of Tata Motors. Mexion wheels was initially totally dependent on Tata Motor and 70% of its sales revenue was from Tata Motor. The company faced problem of survival during 2003–2004 because of overdependence on one customer and the lowest margins on the product.

With a need for survival and low margins, promoters decided to go for expansion of the plant by adding product portfolio from other customers. Company's turnover was Rs. 50 crore in 2005 and in a span of eight years it had reached Rs 300 crore. Their revenue growth was due to an increased customer base and valuable product portfolio. In the expansion phase lot of recruitment was done to handle production demands from customer. With introduction of new technologies, there was tremendous improvement in operating efficiency.

Organization Structure: During the Start-up Phase There Were Hierarchies of Managerial Levels

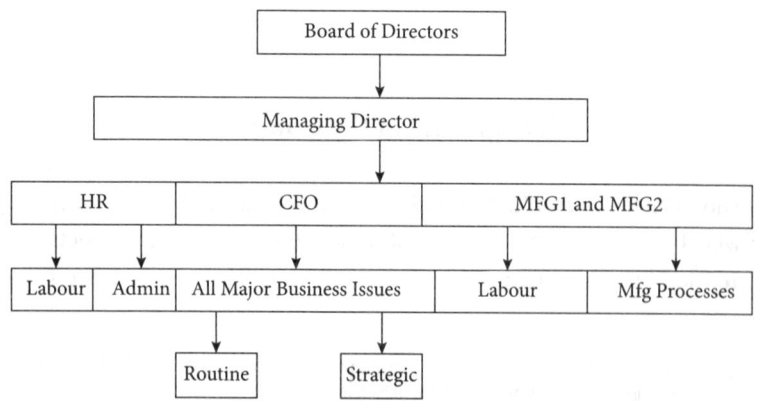

After expansion in car plant business, the management decided to create two strategic business units namely passenger car wheels and heavy-duty vehicle wheels. The plant managers were promoted and assigned as vice presidents for respective business units.

Production Process

The company purchases steel sheet coils and the coils are converted in to wheel rims. Sheet metal cutting, pressing, welding, and assembly are major processes used in manufacturing. To fulfil the demand most of the operations are automated with robotizing few of the operations.

In January 2013 a meeting was called by board of directors to discuss the financial results of the company. The following were the major observations:

1. The top-line growth was as per the expectation and planned expansion. The results were encouraging and a consistent growth of 30% was achieved for the last five years.
2. Company's ROI target was 18% but there was a consistent decline. In 2005 ROI of 18% was achieved but current ROI was 12%. The explanation given by the management for decline in ROI was increase in material prices was not compensated by proportionate increase in selling price.
3. Because of severe competition, margins were reduced and large varieties in small quantities were produced.
4. The board was not happy with the explanation because with investment in technology, manufacturing cost was considerably constant for the last five years. The argument of increased material price does not stand.
5. It was decided to conduct a preliminary audit about materials management and external auditor was appointed to provide insight about the materials management.

The audit findings and observations were as follows:

Truck plant and passenger car use the same system of material accounting but there are deviations in recording of the transactions. The material is issued first and the planning order is issued later.

Production order is issued for okay quantity to be manufactured and material is issued till required okay quantity is produced.

Material reconciliation report is not prepared.

Material scrap % as a percentage of sales is within limits of 3 to 4% but **material usage variance** is very high and it is 10 to 12% of buying cost of material.

Estimated scrap as per BOM and actual process scrap do not match.

Contribution of material in total cost should be 55% as a standard norm of the product but currently it is 65%. The improvements in process cost are wiped out with material variances.

Manufacturing order quantity and material issued is not matching. Material issue and material consumption reconciliation are not available.

Company uses online bid (auction) system for disposal of scrap. The details of the tender offer with prices for last six months of scrap disposal are as follows.

Scrap Item Code	Maximum Rate (Estimated) Rs. per Ton	Supplier (Buyer)	Minimum Rate Rs. per Ton	Supplier (Buyer)	Qty Sold in Tons	% change in rate
PUN 9506 Butt weld, rim scrap	27600.00	Ambika Waste Pvt. Ltd	22200.00	Ambika Waste Pvt. Ltd	528.12	(–)19.56
PUN 9520 Blanking off Cuts	29600.00	ShriyaShristi Association	25900.00	Virani Iron and Steel	705.67	(–)12.5
PUN 9552 Stud Hole	26800.00	Ambika Waste Pvt. Ltd	24300.00	Ambika Waste Pvt. Ltd	27.07	(–)9.328
Pun 9553 Coil Ends	31500.00	ShriyaShristi Association	27000.00	Asia Steel	285.61	(–)14.28
PUN 9539 Punch End Vent Hole	27600.00	Ambika Waste Pvt. Ltd	23600.00	Ambika Waste Pvt. Ltd	455.14	(–)14.49

Some of the important concerns expressed by the auditors were:

The supervisory staff is not aware about the activities in their areas of responsibility. Sitting in the same location there is no effective communication and everybody talks about his limited role in the organization.

The scrap disposal is a routine job rather than a strategic function.

Quality control does not report separately rejection in production system but it is directly transferred to scrap.

There are incidences of negative stocks reported in scrap.

Supplier wise material rejection details are not available.

End piece (waste) scrap is increased.

The entire supervisory staff is young and lack seriousness in decision making.

There is a need to develop a material management and accounting policy.

Auditors report was discussed with top management and all head of departments were present. Following objections were raised by the operative management on the observations of the auditors.

Why we should know what is happening in other departments? Why we should understand their activities?

Material scrap is 3% of sales value so there is not any need for investigation of process performance.

The variance in designed scrap as per BOM and process scrap will be always there because of variation in material size.

Every month we have to dispose of 200 tons of scrap and it should be a routine job and can be handled by junior managers.

Supplier wise rejection report is not required because we buy from leaders from the industry and all incoming materials are as per standards.

The top management is not happy with the attitude of the managers and they decided to appoint a committee to investigate the matter in depth. Role of committee is to design a material management and reporting policy. Committee should design KRA for various managerial positions for optimum utilization of materials. Both strategic business unit heads and CFO jointly should develop an action plan to bridge the gap between top-line and bottom line of company.

Conclusions

The company is not happy with the attitude of the managers in dealing with the handling of the scrap which has a considerable impact on the material and operational cost of the company and is directly impacting the bottom line. The management has not accepted the explanation given by the managers and has decided to appoint a committee to look into the matter in depth. The casual approach of the managers towards the current situation is surprising. It is to be seen what measures the committee suggests and how well it is able to design a materials management policy. It will also be preparing KRA (Key Result Areas) for the managerial positions. How well it will be able to design the policy and KRAs and how will the managerial staff react to it would decide the success of Mexion in the days to come.

Case Questions

1. What according to you is the problem in the case?

2. What could be the possible reason for the casual attitude of the managerial staff towards the situation?

3. If you were made in charge of the materials department how and what materials management and reporting policy would you device? What action plan would you device to reduce the cost and improve profitability of the organization?

11

Racing to Deliver

A Case Study on E-commerce and Logistics

Learning Objectives

To understand the changing preference of Indian consumers towards retail and online shopping. To understand the challenges faced by retailers and online platforms in attracting consumers to shop at their respective platforms. To understand the constraints and challenges faced by retailers and online platforms to sustain in a highly competitive market.

Synopsis

The current case discusses the growing trend of Indian customers towards retail and online purchases. It throws light on the factors that are aiding the growth of retails outlets and the increasing footfalls in these shopping formats. These retail malls are concentrated in 35 to 40 odd cities in India. This growth is fuelled by young couples having disposable income and eager to try out new things. There has also been an increase in online shopping, and this trend is bound to grow at a rapid pace. There has been constant struggle by online platform companies to attract customers from offline to online mode and similarly the retail malls are struggling to get the online customers to shop at their malls. The type of product, the convenience of buying, the ability to touch, feel and see the product, the payment options are some of the factors which influence the consumer to shop online or offline. However there are many constraints like funding and infrastructure that these companies have to face. The

Indian Business Case Studies. Priti Pachpande and Sham Bachhav, Oxford University Press. © ASM Group of Institutes, Pune, India 2022. DOI: 10.1093/oso/9780192869401.003.0011

case discusses how can these companies overcome these challenges and survive in the highly competitive marketplace.

The Brick and Click Retail

These are interesting times for the retail industry in India. Till the end of the 20th century, the way people shopped, where they shopped, what made a certain piece of merchandise desirable, even the rules of engagement between shopper and shopkeeper stayed virtually the same for centuries and then hit a series of transformative curves. A miraculously revived-from-the-dead Shahjehan could have navigated Chandni Chowk of the 1990s with greater ease than a nostalgic beatnik returning in 2015.

The beginning of the 21st century saw rapid growth of the mall culture. People abandoned traditional markets in droves to press their noses against fancy windows of stores with unpronounceable names and scarcely recognisable merchandise in plush air-conditioned comfort. It took a while but both retailers and shoppers grew to love this new way of shopping. Yet, just a decade later, the mall is yesterday's phenomenon and e-commerce is the way the India of tomorrow is shopping.

Same Consumers Online and Offline

The premise of a click versus brick narrative is flawed. The same generation of Indians that is driving the exponential growth of online shopping is also driving the traffic to the major retailing districts across Indian cities. A quick traffic count at any of the leading malls across the top 35–40 cities will reassure that there is no dearth of visitors. Yes, the cash registers are depleted as more and more purchases are diverted to the cheaper prices showcased by e-marketplaces flushing speculative funds into discounts in the hope of creating a habit. To understand the phenomenal success of e-commerce, one needs to start by understanding what modern retail means to India. The one key difference modern retail has made was the breaking of the counter-top and creation of self-navigated aisles.

Modern retail allows shoppers to engage with the merchandise on the shelves, read the pack descriptions, the ingredient stories, the benefit claims, try things on themselves, sample their uses, and judge for themselves the worth a product would add to their lives, the shopkeeper gets reduced to a mere cashier. This empowerment of the shopper is what is stimulating the growth of brick-and-mortar modern retail.

The early years of the 21st century are when the larger cities of India started enjoying the demographic dividend—hordes of young employed singles and affluent young families migrated to aggregations of employment and consumption in a few areas of the cities. This self-confident, self-aware, conscious consumer of branded merchandise started voting with his wallet and led to the accelerated growth of modern retail.

E-commerce has taken this journey of empowerment to the next level. It offers the first level of engagement with the merchandise, the price at which it is available in different shops and the stock position without the mandatory trip to the shopping district. In our traffic, this is surely a huge service. Further, online access to information and buying sites allows shoppers to make their decisions at their own pace rather than be dictated by time and space constraints. In fact, a series of shopper surveys show that close to 90% of shoppers go online at some point in their decision-making process.

This data proves how successful the 'habit change' strategy is already proving. By the same coin, however, only 10% of people make up their mind on what to buy without making a trip to one or the other brick-and-mortar shop! Shoppers continue to be wary of buying merchandise they have not seen, touched or felt for themselves. Indeed, to do so would be to revert to the dark ages of the nineties when one would have to accept whatever was handed over across the counter.

Clearly, while retailers on either side of the e-wall have taken adversarial positions, the shopper has decided to do the smart thing by combining the merits of both click and brick approaches to buying. Customers are checking out products online and buying offline, checking out products offline and buying online—just not with the same retailers. It is up to the retailers to try and extract full value from the shoppers they are engaging in one platform but losing to the other.

Be Present, on Tap

The challenge and the opportunity facing retailers today—of both the brick and click varieties—is to create an integrated platform for engaging the shopper and seeing through the full decision-making process. A platform that would allow the retailer to enter the conversation early in the shoppers' decision-making process, hold his hand through the journey and allow him to close the purchase whenever and wherever he is ready to do it. This would require not just the big brick-and-mortar brands to invest in virtual brand stores but also perhaps require the most successful e-commerce marketplace to create physical retail spaces.

Already today, we see retailers talk of Omni-channel services such as 'click and collect' and 'virtual aisles'. The former allows one to take an online shopper to the physical store while the other extends the merchandise pitched to a shopper already engaged in the physical space. These are mere indicators of the larger concept—to be available to the customer whenever he happens to be in the mood to shop, wherever the fancy strikes him and being able to serve him regardless of whether he is just surfing or reaching for the wallet.

E-commerce an On-Off Affair

There was a time when you went to your local neighbourhood grocer to buy most of what was required. From time to time, a visit was made to shops in the local bazaar for things such as clothes and shoes. And rarely, one would go to a distant or larger city to buy something special. For an increasing number of Indians, those days are long gone. We are encouraged to buy and are constantly being enticed with variety, novelty, sales and flexi payment options. And, we have a number of retail channels to choose from. We can walk down to the nearest shop and pick up something, order from online marketplaces using our mobile phones, laptops, or PCs or even shop using the home shopping channels on TV.

Online modes of shopping are fast gaining traction, in both overall volumes and the product categories. Yet, the person who shops online is the same person who shops offline. So, how does a person decide where he is going to shop, for what and when? What is his or her decision-making process and how is this evolving over time in favour of one channel over another?

A known fact is that, at 65% of e-commerce transactions in 2014, online ticketing continues to have a lion's share of the e-commerce market (according to a CRISIL Research report). The product, the e-ticket, is available to you almost immediately. There is no scope for wrong, damaged or delayed product delivery, no need for touching, feeling or seeing, or checking the size. No need to check usability, how it works. And one is saved long hours of waiting in a queue.

But all products sold online are not this amenable to being bought. Therefore, online marketplaces provide virtual substitutes to the real-life evaluation experience. They bring the product to life through pictures, consumer reviews, comparisons. In fact, a few marketplaces even have an online chat for instant clarification of the buyer's doubts. All this has moved some consumers further into the arms of e-commerce.

Touch and Feel Barriers

Touch and feel factors and high involvement arising from large ticket sizes in certain categories are reasons why most people prefer to shop offline rather than online. In the present scenario, online players are, to some extent, piggybacking on the existing brick-and-mortar stores. Enterprising shoppers go to their nearby brick-and-mortar store, try on items, and then buy online at a discount.

The existing strategy of e-commerce players to deal with touch and feel barriers is of allowing trials and returns. However, this trial option may not be available in all locations. Also, as such companies scale up operations, such strategies may strain their networks at higher adoption volumes. Also, if the trial price is hiked, it may even lower consumer adoption of this feature.

One avenue that Indian online retailers may need to consider is pop-up stores, coinciding with the launch of new products. These stores, which pop up overnight for a few days in a given location, are a common phenomenon in western countries. Consumers try products at the buy them right there, or order online for delivery at a discount.

Online payment is something that kept a section of consumers at bay for some time, but here the e-commerce companies have responded by going the extra mile and offering various payment options.

Cash on Delivery

Credit and debit card payments allow for convenience. Cash on delivery (COD) caters to those who want to receive the product before parting with their money or who otherwise do not want to make online payments. But COD has thrown up some challenges of its own. Collecting and handling large amounts of cash daily is bound to come with some hurdles for e-commerce companies and their logistics partners. Is it possible to move customers from COD to online payments? How does one convince the customer buying from unbranded sellers or for transactions involving large amounts of cash? One option may be along the lines of what Alibaba offers—holding customers' payments in an escrow account. Only when the customer accepts delivery and is satisfied with the product delivered is the money transferred to the account of the seller.

There are many such points in a consumer's consideration and purchase cycle where critical factors push or pull consumers to offline or online. E-commerce companies are hard at work to pull customers their way. At some point, the empire may strike back, and we may see brick-and-mortar retailers in India innovate their shopping experience to woo customers back. This trend has taken root in the more developed markets.

In-store Technology

In-store tablet technology can guide people to choose the right products at right prices. 3-D body scanners are used to customize clothing to ensure the right fit. Kiosks and iPads allow people to browse product ranges and order items while at the store. A retail furniture app allows users to see how a piece of furniture would look in their homes before buying it. Top shop used a live stream of Virtual Reality experience of its London Fashion Week show. Quick response codes can be placed in shop windows, POS and ads and provide more product information. Such and other brick-and-mortar technology innovations may catch up in India soon, before the Indian e-commerce market reaches the same stage of stability as in the West. As digital meets brick-and-mortar, the customer is set to be king. Understanding his or her impulses, habits and preferences will provide the edge to those seeking to serenade him.

E-commerce-focused logistics companies are prepping for a year of hard graft, battling infrastructure hurdles and competition from a new breed of start-ups while also keeping pace with the ambitious growth targets of the country's biggest online retailers. GoJavas, Ecom Express, and Delivery are rushing out a slew of services, expanding their reach and building up technology platforms for clients such as Flipkart and Snapdeal that have set record sales targets for this year. India's online retail market is estimated to reach $36 billion (Rs 2.4 lakh crore) in 2016–2017, up from $11 billion in 2014–2015, according to Goldman Sachs.

The key will be to provide good customer experience by focusing on reliability, speed, and visibility, so that (customers) can keep buying again and again. In trying to access many of these areas, delivery and logistics companies face significant hurdles. The lack of surface transport and limited air cargo capacity act as bulwarks preventing smooth first-mile and last-mile deliveries. Even as the e-commerce segment grew exponentially over the last 2–3 years, logistics continue to be a problem. Also, the high costs and lack of technology innovations have not happened as one would've expected.

This demands that the logistics partners spend more also on strengthening their physical infrastructure and technology platforms to seamlessly integrate these with that of their clients. Technology will help to handle scale, creating software that will help handle updates on the field, swipe on delivery and customer interaction, among others.

Ecom Express, which counts private equity firm Warburg Pincus among its primary backers, is also expanding at a furious pace. 'We're looking to begin (covering) 500 towns and cities by end-December, and 1,000 by the end of the next fiscal year (March 2017),' said Ecom Express. It currently reaches about 300 towns and cities. The Gurgaon-based company, which has about 250 clients, is targeting the eastern and northeastern states, 'which, thus far, have been woefully under-penetrated by logistics and delivery firms due to inadequate infrastructure in these places.' We have 17 hubs and about 700 delivery centres, but are in the process of adding centres in 100-odd cities in Bihar, Odisha, and Jharkhand between now and April. Delivery operates in 350 cities and towns and handles about 20,000 deliveries a day.

Integrating technology is at the forefront of these efforts, from developing specialized software to moving towards complete automation. GoJavas, which has automated the sorting stations at two of its major nodal points, aims to do the same across Mumbai, Bengaluru, and Hyderabad in 6–18 months. These firms also have to battle a growing argument that e-commerce companies need to have in-house logistics arms for cost rationalization and greater control over deliveries. Flipkart recently pumped in Rs 666 crore into Ekart, its logistics business.

When the funding dies up, how long will (e-commerce companies) sustain (in-house logistics units)? Will they have that much traction on their own to run these units? Another worry is the emergence of technology-focused, venture capital backed, hyper-local delivery companies in an already crowded space. Start-ups such as Opinion, Parcelled, and Shadow fax Technologies that have come up in the past year promise to deliver goods to consumers within 30 minutes of an order being placed.

Conclusions

E-commerce has transformed the way business is done in India. The Indian e-commerce market is expected to grow to US$ 200 billion by 2026 from US$ 38.5 billion as of 2017. Much of the growth for the industry has been triggered by an increase in internet and smartphone penetration. The ongoing digital transformation in the country is expected to increase India's total internet user base to 829 million by 2021 from 636.73 million in FY19. India's internet economy is expected to double from US$ 125 billion as of April 2017 to US$ 250 billion by 2020, backed primarily by e-commerce. India's e-commerce revenue is expected to jump from US$ 39 billion in 2017 to US$ 120 billion in 2020, growing at an annual rate of 51%, the highest in the world.

The Indian e-commerce scene has witnessed many upheavals, Walmart has invested in Flipkart, Alibaba in Paytm, and many more deals are expected. Many new players are entering the Indian e-commerce market. In January 2020, Divine Solitaires launched its e-commerce platform.

Many online players are setting offline stores, In February 2020, Flipkart set up a 'Furniture Experience Center' in Kolkata, its first offline presence in eastern India. Also many offline stores are setting up their online presence. In May 2020, chocolate maker Hershey India partnered with Swiggy and Dunzo to launch their flagship online store in order to increase reach. Thus there are many happenings in the market to reach out to the customers. It will be interesting to see how the customer's response to these moves of the organizations.

Case Questions

1. With the road conditions as they are today across India and the delays at the toll collection centres the condition of the carrier trucks and the usual habits of the long-distance drivers including overloading will it be possible to reach global targets of delivery within 30 minutes? Even the Pizza delivery commitments are not feasible on crowded roads in cities?

2. What needs to be done to professionally integrate all the stakeholders in the logistics management for e-commerce companies to radically improve the present hurdles which threaten to grow exponentially obstructing all plans even of single-day delivery?

3. Online platforms are planning for offline stores and offline stores are planning for online platforms to beat competition from either of them. Do you think this strategy will succeed? Explain your answers in light of changing preference of Indian consumers.

12

The Wings on Fire

A Case Study on Tata's Acquisition of Air India

Learning Objectives

The case envisages to provide an insight to students, faculty, and management institutes adopting business case methodology as a unique pedagogical feature in the major aspects of mergers and acquisitions involving public and private sector setups. The case on Tata's acquisition of the national carrier Air India is a major trendsetter in disinvestment plans of the government but also exposes the gutsy confidence with which the Tatas look at this as not only as reacquiring a lost crown jewel of the group but demonstrating their will and commitment to restructure and revive the ailing giant of an airline.

The case study would be very much useful for students in strategy management as also in international business as the restructuring and revival post-merger depend heavily on effective strategic restructuring plan and strategic leveraging of resources for international aviation market.

Students of Project Management and Strategic Finance Management would be interested in essential cost control measures as also in achieving financial synergic benefits as a major factor in the revival process equally interesting would be for students in international marketing aspects in

Indian Business Case Studies. Priti Pachpande and Sham Bachhav, Oxford University Press. © ASM Group of Institutes, Pune, India 2022. DOI: 10.1093/oso/9780192869401.003.0012

developing and sustaining competitive advantage in the current VUCA market scenario in international aviation segment.

Synopsis

In its major disinvestment plans present government of India has been trying for more than three years and was not getting a single bidder for disinvestment offer for the perennially ailing Air India the national carrier in spite of sinking more than Rs 65,000 crore for its revival over a decade and causing a continued loss of nearly Rs 620 crores on its operations per month and continuing to bleed the national exchequer Rs 20 crore with each passing day.

However in its continued efforts government succeeded in receiving altered terms of its offer two bids in its recent offer (100% disposal offer of Rs 12,906 crore as reserve price set by the government). One was from the Tatas who bid for an enterprise value of Rs 18,000 crores and the second bid was from a consortium led by Mr Ajay Singh of Spice Jet for Rs 15,100 crores (Rs 12,835 crores towards taking over Air India's debt and Rs 2,265 crores in cash payment). This incidentally is the first major privatization step by the government in nearly two decades.

On 8 October 2021, the Department of Investment and Public Asset Management (DIPAM) Government of India announced that the Tata Sons Ltd subsidiary company Talace Pvt Ltd had won the bid for the national carrier Air India after bidding of Rs 18,000 Crores (USD 2.4 billion) against a reserve price of Rs 12,906 crores (USD 1.72 billion). The other shortlisted bidder was SpiceJet at Rs 15,100 crores (USD 2.01 billion).

Air India, the national carrier for India under the iconic brand name as 'The Maharaja' depicted by the image of an Indian royal host in the typical Indian welcoming style, was quite popular among Indian travellers of the 60s to the 90s with no other competing private airlines in the Indian aviation segment.

However Air India remained a white elephant during major portion of its tenure as a public sector enterprise going from bad to worse as the operating revenue never matching the operating expenses and the huge financial burden of asset aircrafts maintenance costs lease rentals and more nearly 15,000 employees including highly paid pilots and crew members and ground-level staff.

Over a period of decades in spite of the financial support from the government, it turned out to be a major drain on taxpayers money being saddled with huge debts. As at the end of August 2021 the debt had mounted up to colossal Rs 61,000.00 crores.

In fact Air India was regularly listed for disinvestment over previous more than 20 years by the government in power devoid of any firm commitment of its disposal due mainly to sentimental approach in losing a prestigious national carrier, and vested interests lack of clear policy and dearth of interest shown by any local or global buyers.

However over the previous few years it had become loud and clear that the government of India had finally decided and was committed to privatizing Air India and after very long persuasion and pressures on accommodating huge operating losses of nearly Rs 20 crores per day the house of Tatas offered to buy over the ailing airlines through regular bidding process since for Tatas, this acquisition was more than a 'Ghar Wapasi' (getting back to home) of a missing family member.

This deal for Tatas is of special significance since JRD Tata was the original founder of the airlines in the 1950s, before it was officially taken over and nationalized by Indian Government in 1953. For Mr Ratan Tata the chairman emeritus of the Tata Group it marks the return of the family heirloom after a lapse of over six decades. 'Mr JRD Tata would have been overjoyed if he was in our Midst Today—Welcome back Air India' this is how Mr Ratan Tata chairman emeritus Tata sons responded after the final announcement of sale was done by government authorities.

Case Details: Major Terms of the Deal

1. Air India will return to Tatas after 68 years as a national carrier along with its brand and available slots along with the low-cost subsidiary Air India Express and 50% stake in the ground handling firm AISATS.
2. In a nutshell Tatas will acquire 100% ownership of Air India and Air India Express and 50% stake in ground handling arm Air India SATS.

3. Tatas will also get ownership of iconic brands like Air India, Indian Airlines, the Maharaja brands and logos.

4. Tatas will own Air India's 141 aircrafts and over 7000 domestic and international airport slots.

5. Of the bid amount of Rs 18,000 crores the Tatas will pay Rs 2,700 crores in cash while treating the remaining Rs 15,300 crores towards Air India's debt share.

6. The Tatas will also have to pay Rs 9,185 crores towards capitalized lease obligations of 42 leased air crafts—primarily the Boeing 787 Dream liner aircraft.

7. Tatas will retain Air India's 12000-odd employees at least for the first one year of operation.

8. Tatas will have to ensure Air India's business continuity.

9. The new owner is not permitted to transfer (there are at least eight logos) for the first five years of operations afterwards these can be transferred to only to an India entity. In no case this will be offered for sale to any foreign entity.

10. Government of India will retain the residual liability (debts) of Rs 44,678 crores after the deal with Tatas (Rs 46,262 crore debt + Rs 15,834 current liabilities less than Rs 14,718 crore assets plus Rs 2,700 crore cash from Tatas = Rs 44,678 crores). The debts and assets will sit in the books of Air India Assets Holding Company.

11. The deadline for transaction conclusion **ends on December 2021.**

12. It is learnt that the government has signed a share purchase agreement on 25 October 2021 with the Tata Group for the sale of Air India for Rs 18,000 crores.

13. **The Air India's component parts**

The **Air India** group is made of the following components:

1. Air India
2. Air India Engineering Services Limited (AIESL)
3. Air India Air Transport Services Limited (AIATSL—Ground handling Services to the Air India Group and other airlines)
4. Air Line Allied Services Limited (AASL)
5. The Hotel Corporation of India (Centaur Hotels and the Chef air flight Kitchens)
6. Air India SATS Air Port Services Private Limited

The Legacy and Settlement of Outstanding Debts

Air India

The Air India's total debt as of end of August 2021 was Rs 61,562.00 crores (USD 8.21 billion). Of this Tata Sons (holding company of Talace Pvt Ltd) would be taking over Rs 15,300 crores (USD 2.04 billion) and with a cash payment of Rs 2,700 crores (USD 360 million). An estimated amount of Rs 46,262 crores (USD 6.17 billion) will be moved to Air India Assets Holding Ltd (AIAHL), an SPV formed by the government to handle the debt and other non-core assets of Air India such as land and buildings.

Much of the debt is related to the merger between Air India and the other state-owned air carrier the Indian Airlines which was merged with Air India in March 2007. Preceding this the then Government UPA had approved the purchase of 68 aircrafts (from Boeing) by Air India and a year later 43 planes (from Airbus of 320 families for USD 2.2 billion) for Indian Airlines. The Boeing Company also built and transferred a State of Art maintenance, repair, and overhaul facility at Nagpur in Maharashtra. The merger of the two state-owned air carriers in 2007 cost the government Rs 70,000 Crores (USD 9.33 billion) dragging Air India into much deeper financial crisis.

Besides the above debts Air India also owes Rs 16,000 crores (USD 2.13 billion) towards unpaid fuel bills along with other dues to airports and vendors, this is proposed to be moved over to AIAHL for settlement.

Overall it is seen that 75% of Air India's debt will not be taken over by the Tatas except that Tatas will be taking over a debt of Rs 9,000 crores for lease obligations of 40 Air India Jets. The non-core assets including land and buildings of estimated value Rs 14,718 crores will also be transferred to AIAHL.

There are also reports that the government is proposing to add the feeder/regional airline Air Alliance (the second Air India subsidiary) to this mix with a plan to also sell it over. This will result in the government completely exiting the airlines business.

The daily operating losses as of present are around Rs 20 crore per day and from 2010 to date the government has further infused over Rs 1,10,276 crores (approx. USD 14.70 billion) in to Air India (Rs 54,584 in cash support and Rs 55,692 crores in loan guarantees.

The four Air India subsidiaries AIATSL, AASL, AIESL, and Hotel Corporation of India and the non-core assets which include the collection of artwork antiques, Paintings, and artefacts and other non-operational assets have been transferred to AIAHL.

The Possible Synergy

The Tatas already have two airlines which are currently making losses: (1) Vistara—A joint venture with Singapore Airlines Limited 51:41 shareholding partnership and (2) Air Asia India—a low-cost service provider in which Tatas have 84% stake.

Post-merger of Air India the Tatas are expected to hold a share of nearly 26% share in domestic aviation market just behind Indigo with 57% market share.

The Air India deal catapults the Tata Aviation conglomerate in to a big-league player in domestic as also in international aviation segment (will be the largest player from India in international market).

The brand Air India has an instant connect. There will be an additional fleet of 141 aircrafts (117 from Air India and 24 from Air India Express) and will have a widespread domestic and international footprint (over 7,000 slots and codeshare agreements) with significant share of revenue from international operations (the flights from Air India to US are a high point).

There will also be repository claims on bilateral rights which will be much of use in expanding international market coverage including Europe, Africa, and South America. (The Air India frequent flyer programme has nearly 3 million members.)

Besides the combined entity will have the advantage of getting experienced crew, ground staff, and engineers from Air India operations which is also a part of the 26-member global aviation group the Star Alliance.

Air India to Give Wings to Tata's Aviation Ambitions

With the acquisition of Air India the combined fleet of Tata airlines will rise to 217 (Air Asia India and Vistara have 28 and 48 planes, respectively) it will give the Tata Group a formidable presence in the international routes, ensure dominance on lucrative Kerala-West Asia routes, and bring economies of scale through better utilization of assets and common contracting network. With the combined strength of Air India, Air Asia India, and Vistara the Tatas will have nearly 25% of the domestic market.

When it comes to international sector, the airport slots and the traffic rights held by Air India will be a key advantage for the Tatas. Air India Express has a strong presence in south India and the acquisition will give the Tatas a large share of the pie in the Kerala-West Asia market. Currently Air India is the only airline from India serving the north American market. Both Air India and Vistara operate their Boeing 787 aircraft in Europe

The Tatas are expected to bring in professional management approach to turn around Air India carry out schedule changes and network optimization and will be focused on consolidation and expansion. Getting the house in order and reduce Air India's losses and expand international market penetration.

Tatas also need to focus on schedule adherence and in-cabin updation. Experts feel that the Tatas should not rush to full merger of its airlines in to one entity instead should drive synergies through common contracting ground handling and in-flight catering and other common services.

The Tata groups financial stability and long-term business sustainability strategy should act as the best catalyst for reviving Air India and getting the airlines back on its feet. Who knows the Air India acquisition may turn out to be a money-spinner for the Tata Group by driving business opportunities for other group brands such as Starbucks or the Taj Hotel.

Sources indicate that the Tatas are planning to integrate Air India's operations with Vistara to build an international premium airlines and Air India Express would be merged with Air Asia India to straddle the low-cost space. The combined airlines now will have 4,486 domestic and 2,738 international slots across Indian and major international airports.

The initial priority is likely to be a significant restructuring of the entire network wherein Vistara, Air Asia India, Air India Express, and Air India to ensure that the individual airlines do not cannibalize each other and do not cross-sell tickets on each other's platform.

On the Table

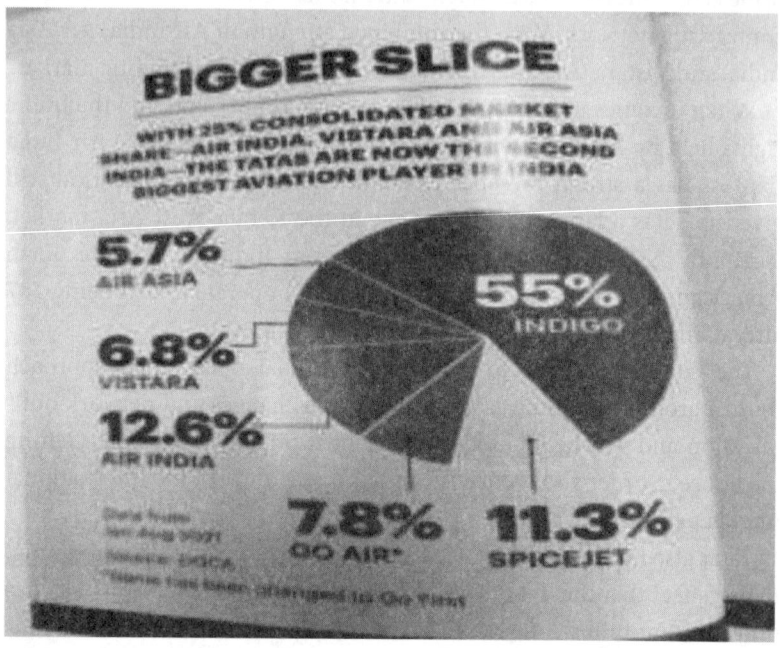

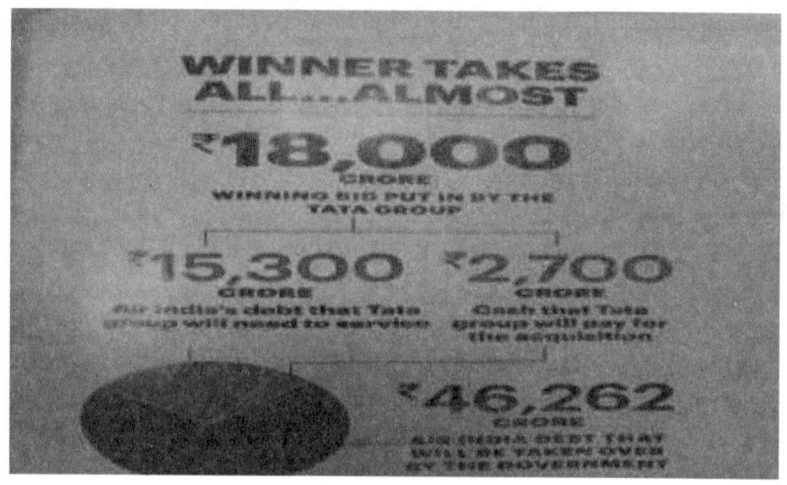

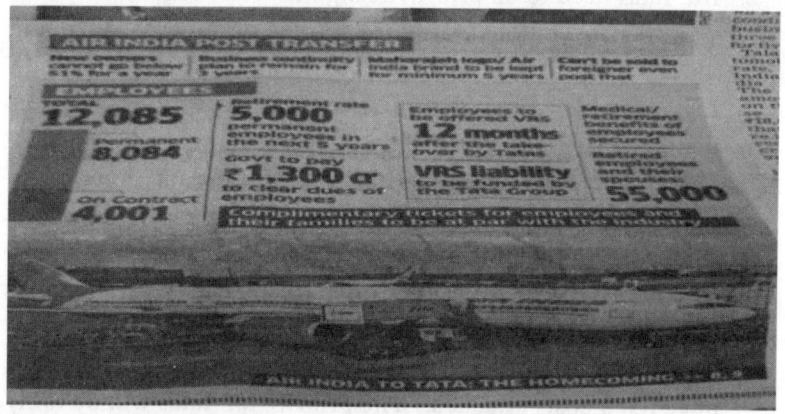

Major Challenges for the Turnaround

The Tata Group will face one of its biggest challenges in its efforts to make the Air India acquisition work given its chequered record in managing major acquisitions in the past, since majority of them are still a work in progress. (Only the acquisition of JLR has been so far one of the better bets.) Tatas will also need to ensure that it has enough bandwidth to spare for accommodating and focusing on this mammoth of a deal of acquiring Air India. Tata's return to civil aviation has been very modest so far through Air Asia India and Vistara (with a reported combined loss exceeding Rs 3,000 crores in FY 2021.) Yet one of the other challenges will be in transforming the culture at Air India. As per an aviation expert there are many unknown unknowns that might make the turnaround much more complex and complicated.

1. Air India unfortunately has been in a bad shape for a pretty long time (2007–2008) and consumer perception of its network and service quality is poor to say the least. The Tatas will assume debt relevant core aviation business with larger chunk of fixed assets remaining with the government. The main challenge for the Tatas will be in reducing the costs by seriously overhauling the MRO— Maintenance, Repair, and Operations.

2. The Tatas need to on priority realign the lease rentals, the route networks and rationalization of surplus manpower. Maximum concessions will have to be derived from the lessors since with Tatas they have now an assurance from recovery of long outstanding debts with Air India. It is estimated that nearly $ 400–450 million will be needed to pay off the lessors and over dues to current suppliers.

3. Almost 30% of the Air India's aircrafts are grounded. It is therefore necessary to infuse additional capital to operationalize these grounded aircrafts which need severe repairs and overhaul. (The grounded aircrafts mean loss of revenue besides huge fixed costs attached.) The priority for Tatas will be to fly all the Air India aircrafts to bring in incremental revenue and cover the costs.

   The initial estimates are that Tatas will need to invest $ 7–8 million to refurbish each of around 50 Air India planes totalling to an estimated outgo to be around $ 400 million. Adding all the above nearly $ 2 billion will be needed immediately over the next few years in to post-merger consolidations.

4. If and if only the Tatas can manage the overall cost structure of the merged airline there is a good possibility that they can reverse the current situation in which the airline is stuck up with losing nearly Rs 20 crore per day.

5. Tatas need to leverage and synergize the turnaround efforts by involving other group companies such as TCS with all the networking programmes as also the Indian Hotels of the group on the catering services. This of course needs to be monitored carefully since the global competitors are already far ahead in engaging latest technology and customer experience in the operations. It is expected that Tata group will be more agile to face competition effectively given their technological prowess, supply chain management, resource allocation route selection, and modernization of the fleet. (Tatas will have access to existing network, overhaul aircrafts skilled pilots, and maintenance staff—All this without any interventions from the government.

The Tata-Air India

Integration Process Has Already Begun at Tatas

As the first step in the integration process it is reported that Tata Sons have setup a short-term advisory team comprising Tata Group Executives including board members. Global Aviation specialists and some top Air India officials to discuss on priority the integration strategy for Air India merger with Tatas to work out the funding plans. Tatas also are considering raising Rs 15,000 crore through a syndicated loan of three years maturity to support its funding for AI acquisition. State Bank of India is expected to be the lead banker with consortium of standard chartered. CITI bank and few more foreign banks as the need be.

As is known Tatas have already created a wholly-owned subsidiary Talace Ltd which made the bid on behalf of Tatas. Already set in motion are selection and appointment of a CEO for the aviation business and has assigned Mr Nipun Agarwal Tata Sons Senior VP for consultations with Air bus/Boeing. Tata is keen to hit the ground running with the two airlines already in its stable Vistara and Air Asia India and will formulate and is committed to execute its overall integration strategy for post-Air India acquisition as per its specific strategic plan.

And for Tatas with Air India in its basket is yet another start of a long journey ahead we need to wait and watch the integration process to succeed as expected.

Conclusions

1. The government's decision to disinvest Air India was driven not by its right-wing ideology nor by classical economic theories of principle agency costs but by hard reality of its fiscal imbalances and the innately uncompetitive business model of Air India in highly competitive global airline industry.
2. On the hindsight Tata Group is perhaps the best possible revival opportunity for Air India in the present circumstances. Tatas have the

management depth, political clout, and financial stature to garner resources necessary for the wide-ranging restructuring exercise for Air India in its stable of large conglomerate of units in major segments of the market.

3. It is also a matter of facts that Tatas themselves are a debt-laden group with its huge capital requirements to emerging dislocations in its automobile and power businesses both of which have massive debts and negligible profitability. In any well-governed group this is ultimately bound to create conflicts over capital allocations.

4. For Air India now a Tata Enterprise regaining its pride of place as an internationally competitive commercial airline company would be the true measure of success in mitigating its wings which have been on fire for decades. It should be able to rise up like a phoenix once again from the ashes.

Case Questions

1. After a lapse of nearly 12 years the Tata Group is attempting a major acquisition in the aviation segment primarily driven by its sentiments towards Air India which at one time was one of its crown jewels. But there is long gap of nearly eight decades which has greatly eroded in value terms its own financial strengths due mainly to miscalculated diversifications and acquisitions difficult to manage. Is it appropriate for Tatas to take over a whale of an acquisition like the Air India likely to derail its empire from long-term business sustainability?

2. Considering the ground realities of the deal is fair for the government to deny inclusion of major fixed assets of maximum NPV like the land, buildings, and artefacts of erstwhile Air India which perhaps could be a major catalyst in the resurrection of Air India—Is the deal clear and fair in its terms?

3. Both the parties seem to have disregarded the fundamental principles of business economic considerations while finalizing the

terms of the deal at the outset it appears like a conjuncture of help-lessness of the government and being overwhelmed by sentiments attached to regain of old crown jewel in Air India by the Tatas. Is this in the long term a strategically correct and guaranteeing purposeful business?

4. Last but not the least: Will Air India's fortunes improve under Tata management?

13

A Good Strategy for Growth?

A Case Study on Merger of Sun Pharma and Ranbaxy

Learning Objectives

To understand the meaning, method, and advantages and reasons of merger and acquisition. To study the impact of regulatory bodies on the business. To understand the corporate strategy, operational strategy, and global strategy of business. To understand the methods of leading the industry with monopoly. To study the value of giant companies in the domestic and international markets. To understand the effect of interference of regulatory bodies national and international on the industry growth and development.

Synopsis

Sun Pharmaceuticals Industries acquiring Ranbaxy Laboratories to be counted as a significant global supplier and leaders of generic medicine. Their deal has been strictly securitized by national and international regulators. Ranbaxy's four plants were prohibited from selling drugs in USA for reporting false data of loss to seek approval from FDA. Ranbaxy being significantly valued was eyed by two equity funds and one MNC apart from Sun.

Ranbaxy's portfolio of India alone was $2 billion and with a merger valued at $3 .2 billion. Ranbaxy's export revenue is already under stress following regulatory woes in the US, the company's biggest export

Indian Business Case Studies. Priti Pachpande and Sham Bachhav, Oxford University Press. © ASM Group of Institutes, Pune, India 2022. DOI: 10.1093/oso/9780192869401.003.0013

market. Sun Pharma's efforts towards resolving Ranbaxy's regulatory issues with the FDA can help the Mumbai-based drug maker reap lucrative results in the coming years. The giant joint venture needs to face the challenge of Competition Commission of India (CCI) approval as it is bigger in assets and turnover than the CCI limit to chalk out an existence in the domestic market.

Historical Background

Ranbaxy Pharma industry is one of the largest Indian companies valued at $2.2 billion with an Indian portfolio alone. If one uses a multiple of seven to arrive at their value. Then there is the company's branded products business in the United States, which is unaffected by the FDA alert. Its over-the-counter medicines, Revital and Volini have combined annual sales of over $80 million. If one uses a multiple of seven to arrive at their value (as was done when Abbott acquired the domestic formulations business of Piramal Healthcare).

Ranbaxy's Legacy

Its four plants have been prohibited from selling drugs in the United States. It reported a false data of consolidated net loss of Rs 186 crore for the quarter ended 30 June, as compared to Rs 524 crore in the year-ago quarter to seek approval of the United States Food & Drug Administration, or FDA, for its generic medicines, and paid a penalty of $500 million to settle the matter in the previous year.

About Sun Pharma

The deal with Sun Pharma values Ranbaxy at $3.2 billion. This company wants to improve its revenue by merger and acquisition of Ranbaxy to lead the pharmaceutical industry in domestic and internal market.

The Synergies

The union of India's two giant drug producers, Sun Pharmaceutical Industries and Ranbaxy Laboratories, have created a blend in the pharmaceutical world with Sun's $3.2-billion all-share acquisition of Ranbaxy has created India's largest pharmaceutical company as well as a significant global supplier of generic medicine. This merger and acquisition deal is under tight scrutiny of several national—international regulators. Everybody wants to know how Sun will turn Ranbaxy around, which has been in pain for several quarters now. Its four plants have been prohibited from selling drugs in the United States. It reported a false data of consolidated net loss of Rs 186 crore for the quarter ended 30 June, as compared to Rs 524 crores in the year-ago quarter to seek approval of the United States Food & Drug Administration, or FDA, for its generic medicines, and paid a penalty of $500 million to settle the matter in the previous year.

In spite of this, there is significant value in Ranbaxy. Apart from Sun Pharma, two private equity funds and one multinational corporation too were eyeing Ranbaxy. Obviously, Ranbaxy made business sense to them. One of the suitors had alleged that Ranbaxy's Indian portfolio alone was worth $2 billion. (The deal with Sun Pharma values Ranbaxy at $3.2 billion.) Its over-the-counter brands (these can be bought from the chemist without a doctor's prescription) Revital and Volini have combined annual sales of over $80 million. If one uses a multiple of seven to arrive at their value (as was done when Abbott acquired the domestic formulations business of Piramal Healthcare), these two together are worth over $550 million. Ranbaxy owns many such products. Then there is the company's branded products business in the United States, which is unaffected by the FDA alerts and is over $100 million in size.

Global Market for Sun-Ranbaxy

Sun Pharma as a combined entity would have revenue of approximately $900 million. These markets would include Russia, South Africa, Ukraine, Romania, Brazil, and Malaysia. The acquisition would also provide Sun

Pharma a global manufacturing base with as many as 47 production facilities across the US, Latin America, Europe, and India.

Detailed Turnaround Plan

Sun Pharma, it is learnt Company, has chalked out a detailed turnaround plan for its new purchase. According to sources, it has prepared a three-pronged strategy which includes:

- Integration of supply chain
- Field force to enhanced efficiency and productivity, resolution of regulatory
- issues and higher growth through synergy in domestic and emerging markets.

However, sources say the company is targeting a three- to four-year period after the closure of the transaction to engineer the full turnaround of Ranbaxy. Sun Pharma is expecting to close the deal by December 2018.

The Challenges

'The merger of the functions of two companies of this size could be a major challenge. The first step will be to streamline and rationalize functions. While the basic structure and functions could be managed in the first year itself, to turn around the merged entity and to ensure contributions from the buyout will take at least two to three years,' says a pharmaceutical industry insider.

The Sun–Ranbaxy has a challenge to seek approval from CCI with combined revenue turnover exceeding the CCI limit.

Merger Strategy: An Expert Advice

Sun Pharma is also learned to have hired McKinsey & Company with a mandate that includes integration, rationalization, and optimal capacity utilization. The consultant has been given four months to carry out the required exercise at Ranbaxy in order to ensure a smooth merger.

Except for the staff at the ground level, many senior executives of Ranbaxy had already quit after the acquisition was announced earlier in the year. 'They will have to right-size at all levels but it may not happen so randomly in the factories or with the field force,' quoted by senior official at a consulting firm.

Man Power Planning

Currently, Sun Pharma and Ranbaxy employ around 14,000 people each. Experts say that given the current revenue contribution from Ranbaxy with respect to its employee cost, Sun Pharma would be required to immediately correct its staff-production ratio in order to keep employee cost in check once the merger is completed. Ranbaxy's export revenue is already under stress following regulatory woes in the US, the company's biggest export market.

However, reducing staff strength may be challenging for Sun Pharma as rationalizing workforce at the grassroots has the potential to trigger labour unrest and needs to be handled carefully, say experts.

Operational Strategy

An important element of the merger will be to avoid overlaps across departments. Industry sources say reorganization efforts, procurement, and supply-chain efficiency along with integration of support functions could be achieved in the first year itself, while revenue growth in India and other emerging markets, field-force productivity and R&D productivity would yield contributions from the second year onwards.

Regulatory Strategy

A major upside from the deal could be for Ranbaxy's product portfolio. Though many of the first-to-file applications of the company are pending in the US, they have the potential to give a major boost to revenues once approval comes through.

Sun Pharma's efforts towards resolving Ranbaxy's regulatory issues with the FDA can help the Mumbai-based drug maker reap lucrative results in the coming years. Estimates show after the completion of the proposed transaction, the merged entity would have a market share of 9.2% in India and will have leading position in many therapeutic segments like analgesics, gastroenterology, gynaecology, cardiovascular diseases, and neurosciences. However, the two companies will also have to streamline their product portfolios and field forces, as it is likely there will be an overlap here.

Markets after Merger and Acquisition

Industry estimates also show that in emerging markets, Sun Pharma as a combined entity would have revenue of approximately $900 million. These markets would include Russia, South Africa, Ukraine, Romania, Brazil, and Malaysia. The acquisition would also provide Sun Pharma a global manufacturing base with as many as 47 production facilities across the US, Latin America, Europe, and India. Also, with Daiichi Sankyo becoming a 9% shareholder, Sun Pharma can access its pipeline of branded products. Industry analysts are hopeful that Ranbaxy's EBIDTA (earnings before income, depreciation, taxes, and amortisation) margin can be expected to grow in the range of 15–16% once synergies between the two companies accrue in the third year.

Regulatory Challenges for Being a Monopoly

The Sun-Ranbaxy merger makes for a robust case for an anti-trust investigation by the CCI. The current rules require a combination or a merger and acquisition to seek approval from CCI if the combined assets of the enterprises are worth more than Rs 1,500 crore or if the turnover is more than Rs 4,500 crore in India.

The CCI approval is also mandatory if the companies have assets outside India, or their combined assets are worth more than $750 million

(Rs 4,566 crore), or if their turnover is more than $2,250 million (Rs 13,700 crore). With a combined revenue of over Rs 25,000 crore, the Sun-Ranbaxy deal clearly crosses the exemption threshold under CCI rules. However, experts suggest, the approval may not come easy, given that CCI's primary mandate is to keep a tab on anti-competitive practices.

Both Sun Pharma and Ranbaxy are leading pharmaceutical companies in the domestic market. Industry estimates show there are at least two dozen medicines where the market share of the Sun-Ranbaxy combine is significantly higher than the 15% threshold limit provided under competition law.

Case Questions

1. Ranbaxy with a legacy of its separation and alleged misappropriation of business details followed by case suits in global courts have found a great opportunity to dispose of its assets to Sun Pharma a reputed global pharma company. How do you weigh the financial synergy against the bad will (as opposed to good will) of Ranbaxy?

2. Do you feel that the shareholders and stakeholders of Sun Pharma should have vehemently resisted this acquisition of an allegedly tainted company-lest the acquisition works as Millstone around Sun Pharma prospects?

3. Do you think for Sun pharma will this work out to be a good growth strategy?

14

Transformative Turnaround Strategy

A Case Study on Mahindra & Mahindra's Successful BPR Exercise

Learning Objectives

Many companies in the transformative adopt transformative strategies to prepare themselves for future situations in product, process, and market and overall business environments as contemplated. Business process reengineering is a globally proven methodology used to plan and execute effective business turnaround strategies. Mahindras have planned and executed a very successful business transformative strategy through implementation of systematic Business Process Reengineering (BPR) across all its core business units and this case study attempts to explore this success story.

Synopsis

This case will examine the reason behind M&M decision to implement a Business Process Re-engineering (BPR) programme and the benefits that BPR programme can offer to an organization with effective implementation. This case will elaborate on the concept of BPR and the steps that need to be taken to ensure the success of such initiative.

The Case Details

It was in the beginning of 1994, that the senior executives at M&M Nasik unit, started to hear a near whispering news about a major change of

Indian Business Case Studies. Priti Pachpande and Sham Bachhav, Oxford University Press. © ASM Group of Institutes, Pune, India 2022. DOI: 10.1093/oso/9780192869401.003.0014

guards at the top level of the organization, which would mean to many, a near radical change in the styles of management, especially since there was no one being recruited from outside, but persons known to all from the same group, shifting over to new assignments across the group companies. This was supposed to be the first major restructuring exercise in the history of the M&M group, over a very long period of time. This whisper got louder and stronger day by day and in May 1994, a long meeting at the group head office at the Gateway building in Mumbai, between the board members and the CEOs of different group companies, let the 'cat out of the bag'. And a major restructuring of the entire group not only of the senior level executives but also of the vertical restructuring at the business levels was decided.

Thus came the renaming of the SUV (the Jeeps division) division, as the Auto Sector and the tractor division as the Farm Equipment Sector, the other units were clubbed into relevant sectors with clear product and operational level responsibilities. Simultaneously, the major 'strategic objectives' of the restructuring were also communicated to the concerned across the group companies. Basically the two sectors, the Auto Sector and the Farm Equipment Sector underwent major reshuffles at the very senior levels, each sector headed by an ED, like the ED- Auto Sector and ED-Farm Equipment Sector, etc.

The major objectives of the restructuring were to define and formulate, separate business strategies for each of the sectors, based on individual core strengths and critical business drivers versus available as also potential success factors (CSFs). The overall objective being rationalization of group activities towards achieving excellence at the sectoral performance. These objectives in business terms translated as:

1) Achieve leadership position in each of market segments, in which M&M is a player of prominence.

2) Set out sectoral targets for maximizing operational efficiencies and ROI.

3) Streamline operational systems to achieve world-class operational standards in productivity, quality, costs, and customer satisfaction indices.

4) Achieve growth in all business sectors through diversification, new products, and technology infusion. Also look out for opportunities

for inorganic growth through M&A possibilities, which offer reasonable synergy and integrative benefits in the long-term business prospects, both in domestic as also global markets.

5) Develop and implement an HR policy aimed at achieving excellence in management skills, providing optimum autonomy to enable growth in career opportunities inside M&M group. Along with the performance—appraisal include potential—evaluation, for the succession planning across all sectors of M&M businesses.

The above group-level objectives were required to be translated for each sector. The concerned ED along with his business heads were required to prepare broader proposals and related budgets of estimated costs and timelines along with business prospects for the perusal and approval of the MD and concerned board members as required. A broader plan for the Auto Sector could appear as follows:

1) Undertake a comprehensive BPR at the operational level to create Product Units (PUs), as enabling centres of excellence in performance parameters as per benchmarked global standards. The PUs are required to develop and implement, product-focused strategies to achieve benchmarked levels of performance in line with objectives as set out for the sector (M&M, Auto Sector, took consultancy services of M/S Lucas of UK for BPR implementation).

2) Implement TPM, TQM, to enable radical improvements in all the operational levels in terms of productivity, product quality, performance reliability. To focus simultaneously on optimizing the cost of operations to benchmarked standards.

3) Restructure the plant level organization to reduce levels of hierarchy to the optimum structure which would enable faster decision making, and ensure effective, cross-functional, teamwork across the unit level operations.

4) Select and introduce an appropriate ERP system for data analysis and availability, across functions and to streamline all systems and procedures at all operational levels, enabling quicker and relevant discussions and decision making (M&M selected SAP).

5) Develop and adopt improved approaches to IR situation by promoting workers participation in the various shop level projects,

including layout modifications, multi-skilling activities, TPM and TQM projects, productivity improvement plans. Develop a sense of belongingness of all employees in the organization through 'share and care' approach while handling all IR related issues.

6) Explain periodically the business-related environmental issues through meetings and notices for the information and understanding of employees at all levels. Conduct periodical wage revision negotiations with the union in a spirit of 'fair and firm' and transparent approach.

7) The JV with Ford Motors to be launched at M&M to be fully utilized to build world-class business skills at the operational level by adopting the concept of 'Factory inside a Factory' whereby M&Ms could adopt state of the art techniques of operations management not only to improve its existing operations but also for most of the future products and projects implementation activities. (The opportunity of JV with Fords has extensively benefitted M&M in providing exposures to its middle and senior-level executives to work directly with the Ford Executives and visit various Ford factories elsewhere in the world.)

8) The BPR, TQM, TPM, the Ford JV helped M&M to develop its own MMS (Mahindra Manufacturing System) as a forerunner for all its projects. Besides M&M involved all its major vendors also in the adoption of MMS, leading to implementation of 'Strategic Sourcing' aimed at rationalizing the supplier base as also resulting in the steep reduction in the cost of its procurement activities. The steps are taken as above resulted in improvements in each and every aspect of operations at the Auto Sector (of course similar and simultaneous restructuring projects were implemented for the Farm Equipment Sector as well) including, strategic approach to new product development, modernization of infrastructure and process technology, market research, and customer relations management.

'It is however pertinent to note that the Turn-Around exercise was not Under any duress of loss in revenues or product failures or any other obvious reasons.

Before this project was under taken the group was in perfect good health with reasonable revenues and profits.

We need to credit the entire results to the proactive approach of the group to visualize, likely risks and opportunities form short and long-term perspectives of the market scenario for the entire groups' survival, and achieving sustainable momentum in business growth.' The turnaround and restructuring strategies have resulted in major breakthrough such as:

1) Design, development of the highly successful 'Scorpio' model in the SUV segment, which has created a new platform of vehicles in like the 'Xylo' and many more versions of four wheelers from the Mahindra stable.

2) Establishment of world-class, body shop, painting, and assembly and testing facilities in house which gives the organization a competitive advantage and the flexibility in its process choice for products for different market segments.

3) One of the major transformations achieved through this restructuring exercise is the emergence of a 'Learning Organization' wherein every employee has a deeper sense of attachment and belongingness towards his role as an employee and is ready to undertake what it calls for the progress of the organization. (A concept similar to 'Self-directed Work teams' in fact better known as Self Directed Organization.)

4) The tremendous strides made by the house of Mahindra in the product range and overall growth in each and every market segment, and the nail-biting takeovers of both allied and not so aligned businesses such as the game-changer Satyams takeover in the IT sector, and the JVs with the Kinetic Engineering for two-wheelers, world-class 'Navi Star' for the commercial vehicle segment, the 'REVA' JV with the Maini's for electric and hybrid four wheelers, investments in the aerospace industry by acquiring management control in an Australian unit, and many more acquisition plans in the pipeline.

Conclusions

Truly M&Ms' is a real story of enviable growth in all aspects of the group business. This case offers both concepts of 'retrospect' and also 'prospects' for current business.

Those engaged in strategic management and corporate planning along with the critics of Indian entrepreneurial capabilities to sit up and take notice of the possibilities in organizational developments, achievable through mobilizing and electrifying the human resources to achieve success in spite of the mountainous obstacles.

It is very difficult to make even a rough guess as to attribute possible size scenario of the Mighty Mahindra's (M&M to be appropriate) in the years and decades to come in the global business. As the MD of M&M says in all its recent endeavours to grow, and mention that they are not arrogant nor over confident but doing things as per their normal plans and gut feels.

Case Questions

1. What is it that you see as the CSFs of the M&M's, which have enabled them to succeed in most of their strategic plans for growth and sustainability.

2. Having seen the speed with M&M is crossing physical boundaries, including those which are not covered in the above case, do you feel M&M should pause awhile for consolidation of their business status before they venture out for many more new acquisitions and JVs?

3. What remedies do you suggest for the organization to sustain the organizational culture of learning organization, likely to be threatened due to rapid business growth, through JVs and M&As, where cultural integration may be difficult?

4. Explain the concept of 'Thought Leadership' if any emanating from the above case study.

15

'One' versus 'Many'

A Case Study on Product Branding

Learning Objectives

In the present scenario of cut-throat competition, organizations implement different marketing strategies. Branding or brand management is one of the crucial areas, having long-lasting impact on the performance and growth of an organization. The expected learning of the present study is to understand the difference between the umbrella branding, corporate branding, and individual product branding. The objective is to understand the effect of implementation of a branding strategy on the performance, growth, and reputation of an organization. And to learn the branding strategies implemented by the top few companies.

Synopsis

Choice of umbrella or corporate branding as against product branding depends upon the nature and type of the product, how frequent is the requirement of changes in its features, design, etc. Each of the branding strategy has its own merits and demerits. The company has to decide which strategy is suitable for its products and its overall aptitude.

With umbrella brands, one is investing in just a single brand and leveraging its equity across various categories. In the long run, one can economize advertising and new launch costs on the back of this investment. It is not always possible to make the parent brand reach out to every segment or category of consumer. Different sections want different things and one must strategies based on that.

Indian Business Case Studies. Priti Pachpande and Sham Bachhav, Oxford University Press. © ASM Group of Institutes, Pune, India 2022. DOI: 10.1093/oso/9780192869401.003.0015

The Case Study

The standard view of business growth is that growth is always good, bigger is always better and that companies must grow or die. While every company aspires to grow its business, an expanding business brings with it a host of new risks: too many people, too many locations, too many products, and, at times, too many brands to contend with.

At least for marketing managers the choice is clear: they have to decide whether they prefer the simplicity of unified or umbrella branding or the frenetic juggling of a multi-brand portfolio. The choice appears simple but it is not one that can be settled by the flip of a coin, or the roll of a dice. The decision regarding the number of brands to be retained is closely linked to an analysis of the brand's function in its respective market. 'Every market can be segmented, by product, customer expectation or type of clientele.'

This does not mean, though, that a market divided into six segments, for example, should necessarily call for six brands. This depends on their function (do we need endorsing, umbrella, range or product brands?).

Many companies adopt the umbrella branding practice wherein similar or related products are sold under a single brand. The umbrella branding strategy is based on simple logic that the established brand name will create the same psychological impact about the quality, reliability of different products under the brand.

Umbrella branding is a strategy used effectively by some of the largest corporations. They can take success in one product category, and leverage it to launch into an adjacent category, growing revenue.

A company will spend time and money-making people aware of a brand and communicating what the brand means. If an existing product has already done that work, then the investment needed to launch a new product is significantly reduced if the new product can share the existing brand.

There are number of examples of successful business houses using umbrella branding. In Indian scenario we find such successful umbrella brands in every business sector. Following is the list of a few of them.

Samsung, Tata Group, Reliance Communication, Colgate, Lux, Amul, Lifebuoy, Horlicks, Britannia, Airtel, State Bank of India, Life insurance corporation, LG, Godrej, and many more.

Take the case of Marriott Hotels. There is the Courtyard Marriott for business travellers and Residence Inn by Marriott, an extended stay option. Both these sub-brands are endorsed by the parent and yet maintain their own distinguished persona and value proposition in the consumer's mind.

A complete break away from the parent that is the creation of an individual brand would not be possible for Marriott in this case. Primarily because here the consumer is looking for her needs to be met within the universe of Marriott-backed service guarantee. The 'endorsement' is necessary. In effect, branding strategies must be guided by, as well as geared towards, achieving a larger goal.

Let us consider the examples of telecommunications player Tata DoCoMo and two-wheeler major Bajaj Auto, two brands that have chosen to take completely opposite routes around the same time to illustrate the dos and don'ts of the branding journey. And yet, each has valuable lessons in store for future managers.

Choosing My Style

Tata Group's telecom interests cover the entire gamut from GSM to CDMA to internet connectivity businesses. To the layman, this can be translated better by a mention of its brands like Tata DoCoMo (GSM), Tata Indicom (CDMA), and Tata Photon. Yet, two of these three (one completely and one partially) are now defunct. To be sure, the brands, not business interests, are defunct. Mid-2011, the company embarked on an ambitious plan of integrating the three businesses under the flagship of Tata DoCoMo. So out went Tata Indicom and Tata Photon.

Consider this: Total associate retailers of Tata Teleservices is around 5 lakh. Of these, only 1.5–2 lakh were selling recharges for CDMA. Reason: every retailer holds an electronic voucher denomination (EVD) used to recharge customer SIM cards. Earlier, the retailer had to invest in two separate EVDs to be able to offer GSM and CDMA top-ups. And since prepaid is not very popular with CDMA customers (as it is used mostly for fixed lines), few opted for top-ups for CDMA. Post the business integration, the same EVD can be used by retailers to top up both.

A mid-way shift in branding strategy requires enormous planning though and cannot be sprung upon stakeholders suddenly. Sandhu says, 'The company did extensive legwork with distributors and retailers before the branding exercise.'

There were presentations to explain the benefits of the shift as well as bring them on board about the changed protocols. At the company end, there was the integration of the back-end customer support operations for which extensive training was required. Changes were made at every footprint to reflect the integration.

While Tata teleservices chose to leverage its assets by bringing its brands together, Bajaj Auto went on a diametrically opposite path focusing on its sub-brands, Pulsar and Discover. Bajaj Auto, the makers of the iconic Bajaj Scooter, is a leading two-wheeler maker that had always harped on the mother brand Bajaj to transfuse individual product lines with the same values of trust and Indianness.

Rajiv Bajaj officially took over in 2005 when his father, Rahul Bajaj, stepped down after 35 years at the helm. He wanted to create a distinct identity for their motorcycle brands, away from the Bajaj name, which was used far too liberally for everything, from bulbs to electrical appliances to financial services.

'He felt the brand's equity was spreading too thin. The final straw came in the form of the company's hyped XCD (Exceed) brand failing to cut ice with consumers around 2007,' says an observer.

The company suffered its worst setback during this period when its sales dropped 23% (market leader Hero Honda had recorded a growth of 12% that year) in 2008–2009. Since then, the company has studiously followed a two-brand approach, focusing on Pulsar and Discover.

It has dropped the name Bajaj from all communication and those associated with the brand say that nothing would make Rajiv Bajaj happier than the two brands making their mark without the backing of Bajaj.

Bajaj Auto's marketing strategy is something of a cross between sub-branding and individual (or multi-), 'The strategy of Bajaj Auto is different than that of other two-wheeler manufacturers in India. For other two-wheeler manufacturers the sub-brands are model names. For example, Hero manufactures the following 100cc bikes HF, Splendor, Passion. These are model names. It manufactures many such models.

Bajaj Auto, follows a strategy of creating categories. Hence, Pulsar stands for sports bike. Discover stands for commuter bikes. Under each of these categories there are multiple models (like Pulsar 150, Pulsar 180, Discover 4G, Discover 5G, etc)." Each of these models, in turn, targets a different consumer segment. The Pulsar 200NS, for instance, is a state-of-the-art model targeted at the higher end of the consumer spectrum; whereas the Pulsar 135 is targeted at the fresh college graduate who is price- and image-conscious.

'A brand has to have two things TG (target group) and a promise. When the sub-brands are so distinct in their promise and have such distinct TGs, the individual strength and positioning of the sub-brands have to be focused on, independent of the larger umbrella under which they fall. We're going the FMCG way by doing this,' says Bajaj.

The two approaches, experts concur, are in line with the theoretical approach to the subject. 'Telecom is quite commoditised today. People are looking mainly at tariffs and network quality. There isn't much variation in this category. So bringing together multiple brands and leveraging the equity across the board works well for the company (Tata DoCoMo),' says Jaiswal.

Association with an umbrella brand brings with it a certain amount of limitation in the form of certain sensitivity to the group DNA. It can be tongue-in-cheek for sure but not offensive. 'Any advertising must carry a sense of responsibility.'

Given its backdrop, Bajaj Auto might be correct in its new approach of defining the value proposition of its brands and distinguishing them in the minds of the consumer. However, it has not been able to shake off the 'Bajaj' association altogether. 'The ambition of Mr Bajaj of separating the Bajaj from Pulsar and Discover is lofty and to a certain extent impossible to achieve,' says a marketer previously associated with the brand.

'Auto as a category signifies an investment close to the consumer's heart. He wants a reassurance of quality and trust. And he needs something larger than a Pulsar and Discover for that.' He also points out that automobiles be they two- or four-wheelers aren't exactly a one-time purchase-and-forget-it kind of a product category. 'It is not like a shampoo or soap that you buy, use and move on. In automobiles, there are company designated showrooms, sales personnel, service centres all these touch points represent Bajaj Auto and not a sub-brand,' he adds.

Whether they pick the umbrella or sub-brand route, marketers must note that it will never work in isolation, especially for high involvement categories. There will be certain interdependence. Like a Tata DoCoMo may be an umbrella brand from its vantage point. But from a conglomerate point of view, it is a sub-brand itself, drawing on the Tata equity. Similarly, Pulsar and Discover cannot break their umbilical cord with Bajaj completely ever.

Conclusions

When you use corporate branding, you need a general message. Since the brand is company-wide, it needs to capture everything that your company stands for. It needs to capture the spirit of your company in your marketing materials. The corporate branding marketing message needs to not only be strong but also widespread for your customers and your stakeholders.

When you use product branding, the messaging is narrower. You will want your brand to extol the qualities of your product. You will also want your product brand to stand out from other similar products in the market. Whatever you go for, however, the focus of your branding at the end of the day is the product. The product is the centre of your marketing efforts.

Choice of umbrella or corporate branding as against product branding depends upon the nature and type of the product, how frequent is the requirement of changes in its features, design etc. Each of the branding strategy has its own merits and demerits. The company has to decide which strategy is suitable for its products and its overall aptitude.

In case of corporate brand or umbrella brand the company wants to go in one direction over a longer period of time, whereas product branding gives importance to change and expected to be evolved with the market. Refreshing and revising is expected when one chooses product branding as an option Whereas stable reputation over a longer period is expected in the choice of corporate or umbrella brand.

Case Questions

1. In product promotion and marketing strategies what really decides the approach to product branding—is it the product/market preference or the organizational growth strategy?

2. As a customer, how would/should one transit from umbrella branding to product branding in terms of his/her preferences to the buying need?

3. A combination of umbrella brands and product brands would this serve specific market segments to retain customer loyalty and preference?

16

E-mobility—From the Current to the Future

A Case Study in E-automobility

Learning Objectives

Innovative ideas in the field of automobile sector will come up with new solutions to reduce the atmospheric pollution and maintain a healthy environment. The implementation of electric vehicles (EVs) with affordable prices can increase the sales in the market. The heavy charges paid on import of fuels and service taxes can be minimized up to a certain limit. The same amount of money can be utilised for charging centres of EVs.

Synopsis

When one looks back at the year that went by and what it meant for EVs in India, it largely epitomized chaos and confusion on the policy front. It was a time when fence-sitters were still wondering if it is the right time to get into the EV business. However, some of the old diehards like Sun Mobility.

Hero Electric and Mahindra & Mahindra continued to fiercely pursue their passion as if they had already factored policy indecisiveness into their strategies!

It was also a year when start-ups such as Ather, Zoomcar, Vogo, and Lithium Balance aggressively ventured into the development of differentiated products as well as into smart connectivity, bike sharing/rental, bike taxis, and deliveries. New and big names from unrelated businesses right from the Essel group and Modis to the Mittals and Kalyanis also brushed the fringes of the EV arena with their foot-in-the-door strategies.

Indian Business Case Studies. Priti Pachpande and Sham Bachhav, Oxford University Press. © ASM Group of Institutes, Pune, India 2022. DOI: 10.1093/oso/9780192869401.003.0016

The initiative by the state-run Energy Efficiency Services Limited (EESL) deserves special mention for the right intentions but not so right planning. Entry-level electric cars are not meant to run for long distances and rough/tough usage and that's what these cars ended up being subjected to, prematurely calling off the experiment.

With oil prices on the rise and pollution becoming a huge challenge to contend with in some big cities, the clamour for EVs as a solution for clean air got louder. While Karnataka and Telangana announced big fiscal sops to promote EVs, other states like Maharashtra, Uttar Pradesh, and Punjab followed suit with a lot of noise but no serious follow-ups. Some like Delhi were late risers but had no choice but to join the bandwagon when November pollution levels went out of control and they came up with grandiose ideas. Others have still to rise to the occasion and do their bit in cleaning up the environment.

The Policy Front

Even if the policy front was confusing, it wouldn't be fair to label the efforts of the decision-makers as random or erratic. Six ministries (and dozens within them) were continuously wracking their brains to find the right solution for putting e-mobility on the high growth trajectory.

Needless to add, there was extensive lobbying by those with vested interests. Despite all this pressure, the people entrusted with the policy did indeed give their valued inputs that were practical and rational. By the end of the day, good sense prevailed and the latter part of 2018 saw a positive and cohesive thought process emerging on how India should promote EVs. While the year that went by could be summed up as one of cautious optimism, 2019 could be a turning point for e-mobility which could see a slew of innovative ideas.

These include the green number plate, special licences to allow youth in the age group of 16–18 to ride electric two-wheelers, exemption for permits for EVs in commercial space, experimenting with a few thousand electric buses, allowing e-bike taxi operations, and many more. In the electric space, two-wheelers and e-rickshaws are the fastest growing, followed by e-buses and e-cars. Nearly 1.1 lakh two-wheelers and over three lakh e-rickshaws were sold in 2018.

Radical Ideas Required

One of the bold, yet fiercely opposed ideas is to levy a graveness on IC-engine two-wheelers based on the 'polluter pays' principle. This is intended to create a fund that will help in bringing down the cost of electric two-wheelers for a year or two in order to put the first million on the road. Though a welcome step for EVs in India, implementing will need a lot of guts.

The next logical step is to start a massive awareness campaign that will sensitize the general public about the advantages of EVs. Creating simple and basic charging infrastructure will further give a thrust to their acceptance. Bike-sharing and rentals will also help towards the cause of lower pollution and traffic congestion.

Reducing the GST levels both on lithium-ion batteries and EVs will help in making them more affordable. Likewise, mandating a certain percentage of e-bikes for use by courier services, food delivery services, and e-commerce companies will help spread the word on electric mobility.

The EV industry has been working relentlessly towards the creation of a greener future and robust e-vehicle economy. It is important for the industry and policy-makers to work in tandem and help increase their use in India. Eventually, it is the end-user who will need to appreciate the need for clean air and gradually wean away from fossil fuels while buying vehicles.

The Real Challenges and Barriers to Going Electric

Despite the woeful lack of pointers in the direction of electrification, it would seem that the age of EVs is still due to arrive on our shores within the next few years. Not because of the Government's ambitious targets for the next decade and the steps being taken to realize them, but simply because the automobile industry believes that India too will follow the low-carbon footsteps that are being taken by the other big car markets of the world such as China, US, and Japan.

Every major car-maker existing and planning to enter our market is getting into the act. So, while Tata and Mahindra already have EVs in their portfolio (though in very small numbers), Maruti Suzuki, Ford, Hyundai, Toyota, and even Kia and MG Motors are all testing and planning to launch their own EVs within the next few years.

None of these manufacturers are delusional about the mass market prospects for EVs, but they are hopeful that the policy push from the Government will translate into concrete steps that will eventually make EVs attractive even for buyers in the lower price segments. But, apart from range anxiety and the lack of a charging infrastructure, here are a few factors that will determine how the segment will fare in the country.

Incentives

EVs are at the cusp of breaking out into the mass market worldwide. As yet, they constitute a very small niche and are all loaded on the top of the premium price segment. But even there, adoption has been heavily dependent on incentivizing purchases. This is the scenario worldwide including markets like China and the US where the number of EVs on the road are gaining critical mass. Says CV Raman, senior executive director (Engineering), Maruti Suzuki India, 'In these countries too interest in EVs plummet if incentives are withdrawn. Adoption in India too will be heavily dependent on Government incentives'.

Offering an alternative view, Shailesh Chandra, president, Electric Mobility Business and Corporate Strategy, Tata Motors says, 'Yes, demand incentives can help in the short term. But, in the next five-six years, with the expected reduction in battery prices and the simultaneous increase in cost of ICE (internal combustion engine) vehicles due to stringent emission regulations could help EVs offer an inherent operating cost benefit and make them sustainable even in the absence of incentives.'

Cost of the Battery

Currently, the cost of the battery and power electronics constitute almost two-thirds of the cost of an EV.

The most widely used battery materials today are nickel-metal hydride (NiMH) and Lithium Ion (LiON). Multiple factors like demand-supply gaps, uneconomically low volumes, etc., lead to the high cost of manufacturing EVs. Raman points out that an EV's battery, power electronics, and motors can together cost as much as six to seven times that of an IC engine. So, the ex-showroom price of an EV will still be heavily dependent on the cost of the battery pack.

New battery manufacturing capacities are coming up in India and the localization push will help lower costs of EVs just like it does in the case of IC engine cars. Tata's Sailesh says that based on their study and discussion with experts in cell manufacturing, the economic size of a battery manufacturing plant is upwards of 8 GWh. So, clearly localization benefits can be accrued only in the long term and with a meaningful penetration and volumes for EVs.

Price Multiple

The biggest hurdle for buyers looking to go electric is the current high price of EVs. For a buyer who is hesitant to choose a hybrid in favour of the equivalent ICE-only car, the nearly 3x price tag of an EV is too much of an entry barrier. The user profile may make a difference to how affordable it would be to operate the EV and so fleet operators with a higher usage profile will be able to recover their investments faster. Both Raman and Sailesh agree that the price multiple between ICE cars and similarly positioned EV can't be more than 1.2x to 1.3x.

But lower-end cars will tend to be more expensive because of the higher cost of the technology spread over a lower price level. Unfortunately, price sensitivity is also higher amongst buyers in the lower price segment. And the cost-of-ownership issue will further affect long-term viability of EVs.

Challenges from the Grid Side

Most often, the EV discussion only veers around the non-existent charging infrastructure and about who will be responsible and when will this come up in India. The other point that is also raised is about how much of the power generated comes from old, coal-fired thermal power plants and about how EVs may well be only displacing the pollution from the cities to the suburbs where these plants are located. But what about the other challenges that the grid may be faced with if and when EVs start becoming mainstream? And what about the price of charging EVs at private charging stations?

Even assuming that renewable and newer, cleaner sources of thermal or nuclear power come on stream within the next few years, there are other factors that will affect EVs. One will be the skyrocketing demand for electricity from a country that is already seeing a surge in demand for consumer electronics and appliances, particularly split air conditioners.

In many cities, the annual increase in demand for air conditioners is in the high double-digit figures. According to Rahul Tongia of Brookings India, the good news, however, is that projections for 2030 show that even with a fair penetration of EVs (two, three and four-wheelers, and intracity buses), the increase in demand for electricity is likely to be only about 100 TWh (Tera watt-hours) or about 4% of the total power generation capacity. So, ramping up power generation should be possible to meet that growth in demand.

But, how about the price per charge for EVs that a private infrastructure operator would need to levy for it to remain profitable? Rahul says that is a more worrying factor where studies seem to indicate that it might have to be as high as ₹15–16 per unit, assuming that input cost of electricity is ₹5 per unit.

Will EVs be economical to operate if each top-up is going to cost that much? Will that lead to a messy situation where people divert electricity meant for domestic use into a commercial network? Will electricity need to be taxed by state governments for them to compensate for the loss in revenue from the drop in sales of fossil fuels? Currently, nearly 3% of the GDP comes from taxes on fuels. These are serious issues that will need to be sorted out.

What Next?

The EV space will also turn out to be like the proverbial 'chicken and egg' situation. But that was the case even with ICE vehicles, where the cars came first and the roads came later. So the charging infrastructure will take its time coming, as will the production capacities for batteries. But, in the meantime, the government needs to also promote hybrids and plug-ins to create an enabling ecosystem for buyers of EVs and those who need to invest and profit from setting up the charging infrastructure.

Conclusions

E-mobility has slowly raised in the market facing the problems compared with the other vehicles. EVs are higher in cost but how can it be managed or affordable to common man. If we want to decrease our personal impact on the environment through transport, then an EV is the way forward. The electric engine within an EV operates on a closed circuit, so an electric car does not emit any of the gases often associated with global warming.

Electric cars are lighter, and—as all of their power is generated from a standing start their acceleration capability can surprise. Petrol and diesel engines can require expensive engine maintenance over their lifetimes—EVs don't. EV is likely to have lower long-term maintenance costs than other vehicles.

The increased popularity of EVs also means more options to choose from for the car itself. There are more affordable electric car options available now than ever before, like the Nissan Leaf and the Renault Zoe, with some of the most popular petrol and diesel models also available in an electric version, such as the Volkswagen eGolf.

Case Questions

1. How much an electric vehicle will contribute in both India's economic and atmospheric growth?

2. What are the other factors on which mass adoption of EVs in India will hinge on?

3. What about the price of charging EVs at private charging stations?

4. What are the challenges that the grid may be faced with if and when EVs start becoming mainstream?

17

What Really Went Wrong with Snapdeal?

A Case Study on Failure of a Promising E-commerce Start-up

Learning Objectives

To understand the business model of e-ommerce platforms operating in India. To understand the importance of consumer sentiments and its impact on company profits. To understand the importance of the competition in the industry and sound financial prudence.

Synopsis

Beleaguered online marketplace Snapdeal is going through troubled breaks. Struggling to raise fresh capital, confuting against internal conflicts, once an e-commerce major Snapdeal has decided to stop all non-core actions, reduce costs, and handover pink slips to employees to turn cost-effective. Earlier Snapdeal was the second best alternative for people after Flipkart but the emergence and rapid growth of Amazon gave people a better alternative. When Amazon entered in 2016 with an additional $3 billion investment in India, it made clear its intention to dominate the Indian market and pose a massive challenge for home ground e-commerce companies, among which Snapdeal became extremely unhappy and didn't keep up the tempo.

Indian Business Case Studies. Priti Pachpande and Sham Bachhav, Oxford University Press. © ASM Group of Institutes, Pune, India 2022. DOI: 10.1093/oso/9780192869401.003.0017

Recently, the brand saw the brunt of Snapchat CEO's 'poor India' comment and lost its brand image due to confusion. Previously the start-up had gone almost through the similar situation; getting blowback from Aamir Khan Controversy. Here, in this case study, we will get to know the mistakes made by Snapdeal, raising a valid question of what is wrong with the Indian start-up.

Snapdeal Founders Admit Their Mistakes—What Went Wrong?

Indian e-commerce portal Snapdeal's management has said it has made mistakes like many of its industry peers, failed in some aspects of its business, which have led to some tough decisions as part of its goal to become a more lucrative business in the next two years.

Execution Errors

Over the last two to three years, with funding coming into the market, Snapdeal like many in the industry started making mistakes, the founders said. 'Has our company and industry been going through a troubled time? Absolutely. Did we make errors in our execution? No doubt about that.'—Kunal Bahl, Snapdeal Founder.

An Imitator in Business

One huge problem with Indian start-ups is that very few companies are true innovators and mostly are copycats. The approach signifies picking up a model working in the US or Europe and to duplicate it in India. They end up putting colossal amount in these business models. This copying approach works really well in China as they are a secured market. The foreign players are banned out there and the economy knows to create replacements. However, India is an open country and players like Amazon, eBay, Uber have a free run to come and here. Thus, a simple copycat strategy is not supposed to work for long.

The brand in its 'exorbitant' rebranding exercise burnt an INR 200-crore hole in its pocket. At a time when the brand was already draining, it tried to look profligate by spending an insane amount of money. They spent a lot of money to shout in the undifferentiated marketplace. 'Branding at the cost of business does more damage to the brand.'

Late Entry into Mobile Payments

Snapdeal has ventured into mobile payments a bit too late with Freecharge Wallet. Paytm's wallet services have already paved their way far ahead. While the market today is full of payment wallets, Snapdeal's failure to grow and best utilize Freecharge's platform has also not gone down well with industry experts and investors.

Snapdeal was under fire with Aamir Khan Controversy: Snapdeal became an unlikely hitting bag for those who were criticizing actor Aamir Khan (Snapdeal's brand ambassador), for his derisive views on the issue of intolerance in India. As a protest against Aamir Khan, many customers took to social media to reveal that they gave poor ratings to the Snapdeal app on app stores, and even majority started uninstalling it from their smartphones.

E-commerce major tried to play safe by saying that, 'It is neither connected nor plays a role in comments made by Aamir Khan in his personal capacity.' Here, the brand was not able to understand users' emotions and the take resulted in mass uninstallation of its app, online shoppers rejecting it. Finally, Snapdeal ended up not showing Amir Khan in its 'Dilki Deal' ad and eliminating the contract. Many users began demanding that they won't buy any product from the e-commerce portal until Aamir Khan gets removed as the brand ambassador.

Departure of Senior-level Executives

There have been several top-level exits in 2016. In January, senior vice-president of marketing Srinivas Murthy resigned. In May, Snapdeal lost its prized Silicon Valley hire Anand Chandrasekaran, who was the brand's Chief Product Officer. In June, the Business Head for electronics, Saif Iqbal, left. In November 2016, Vijay Ghadge, Chief Operating Officer at Snap deal's in-house logistics arm Vulcan Express Pvt Ltd, had quit barely four months after joining the firm.

The management-level exit was of Sandeep Komaravelly in January 2017. He was senior vice-president in charge of Snap deal's zero commission marketplace 'Shopo'. Snap deal's Head of Corporate Development Abhishek Kumar had resigned in February 2017. Tony Navin, Head of Partnerships and Strategic Investments, decided to quit after seven years time. Snapdeal's struggles over the past few months are additionally due departure of a string of senior-level executives.

Drop in Its Valuation

Snapdeal's losses more than doubled to INR 3,316 crore in fiscal 2015–2016, while its revenue growth dropped. Snap deal had posted a 150% increase in losses from INR 1,328 crore in the year ended 31 March 2015.

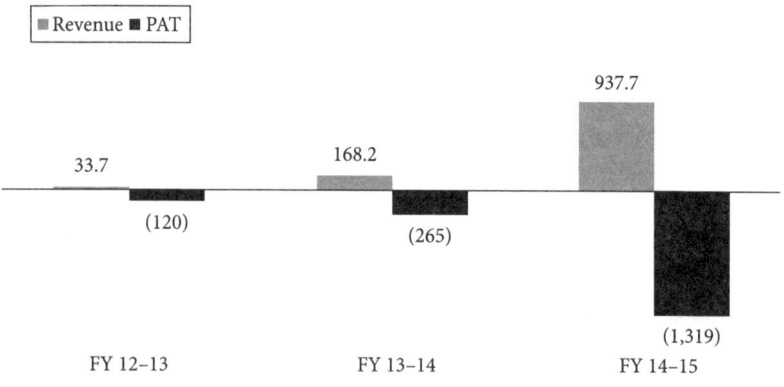

Snapdeal Revenue & PAT (In INR crores)

Revenue grew by 56% to INR 1,457 crore from INR 933 crore in the same period, according to documents.

Struggle in Raising Funds

The company has been struggling to raise fresh funds due to the intense competition with Amazon and Flipkart. Venture capital firms Kalaari

Capital and Nexus Venture Partners, both of which have associates on Snapdeal's board, are in a battle with Soft Bank Group Corp., which has two board seats, over the company's valuation in a potential sale.

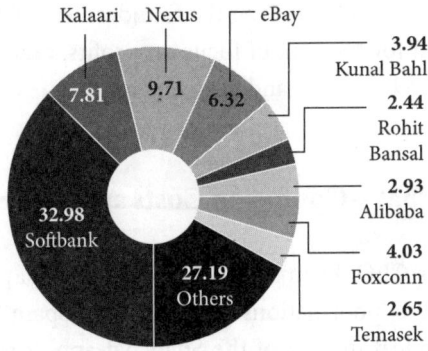

Shareholding Pattern

The board allowed Snapdeal to keep spending, leading to a cash crunch. In July 2016, Snapdeal, which had raised some $1.4 billion since October 2014, still had about $500 million left, after Snapdeal launched INR 200 crore campaigns to transform its image. Discounts and Marketing, at the same time, rejected at least two funding offers because of differences at the board.

Snapdeal Mass Lay-Offs (Cost-cutting Measures)

Snapdeal laid off 500–600 employees amongst its e-commerce market-place, its firms, mobile wallet Freecharge and logistics part Vulcan Express, with '100% salary cut' take. Snapdeal shut its consumer-to-consumer marketplace 'Shopo' recently and disbanded SD Instant, its express delivery service. Categories like beauty and FMCG have been discontinued too.

Kunal Bahl founder of Snapdeal wrote an email, 'with all the capital coming into this market, our entire industry, including ourselves, started making mistakes. We started growing our business much before the right economic model and market fit was figured out.' 'We also started diversifying and starting new projects, while we still had not perfected the first or made it profitable. We started building our team and capabilities for a much larger size of business than what were required with the present scale.' 'Sadly, we will also be saying really painful goodbyes to some of our colleagues in this process,' he wrote without giving the actual number of layoffs. Following the founders' email, Snapdeal is being widely criticized for the lack of focus on profits, excessive spending on advertising and rebranding, and over-hiring.

Snapchat—Confusion Costs against Snapchat

After Snapchat's CEO, Evan Spiegel was alleged of saying that he didn't want to expand to 'poor nations' like India and Spain, people started to down rate Snapdeal instead of the Snapchat app. It sparked off a boycott movement for 'Snapchat' but caught unaware in this storm was the Indian e-commerce portal 'Snapdeal'. Social media users are erroneously downloading Snapdeal app, down rating its services and intimidating to stop using it.

Conclusions

Inventions can't work without a decent business model. Sources claim that Alibaba would enter the scene by merging Snapdeal and Paytm's e-commerce portal. The next trend of start-ups has now initiated. In the backdrop of high valuations and lack of success shown by many players in the e-commerce sector will take a backseat now and many venture capitalist will start to focus on start-ups.

Recent proposal of Flipkart acquiring Snapdeal also fell through due to poor valuation of Snapdeal (Snapdeal's expectation of $ 6Bllion versus Flipkart's offer of $ 1.6 billion. This also was escalated due to Soft Banks Intervention of $ 2.6Billion in Snapdeal which literally drove away Flipkart from acquiring Snapdeal. What is in store for Snapdeal in future is any bodies guess.

Snapdeal has sold its logistics arm Vulcon Express to the Future group in an all cash deal valued at 5.5 million. It has also sold its digital payment platform Freecharge to axis bank for Rs 385 crores. Recently, founders

Kunal Bahl and Rohit Bansal had informed employees that the company has been cash flow positive in June 2018 which means that the company is now earning money from its business. They also claimed that the company has no current or future dependency on funding, has made the industry sit up and take notice.

Case Questions

1. As the e-commerce market is witnessing a fierce competition and since the deal between Snapdeal and Flipkart has failed what do you expect as the next move for Snapdeal? Will Soft Bank's Induction of $ @.6Billion be able to bail out Snapdeal?

2. Being aware of the pitfalls in strategic moves the promoters do not seem to have managed the risks and many decisions seem to be done half-heartedly. Like in case of Flipkart do you suggest a turn-around strategy calling the promoters handing over operations completely to an experienced professional and set strategic objectives for performance?

3. The e-commerce market seems to be consolidating under severe economic stress in the sustenance of operational goals; what business model would you suggest Snapdeal for its resurrection in Indian e-commerce pie?

18

The BSNL Saga

A Case Study on the Collapse of BSNL—The Telecom Company in Public Sector

Learning Objectives

To understand the reasons for the failure of BSNL. To analyse the survival strategies for the PSU. To reflect on the necessity for the existence of PSUs in business.

Synopsis

It is often said that in India 'The government has no business to be in business'. All exercises done by several governments at the centre so far have not been able to see consistent success in majority of the PSUs. The main reason for not focusing on business credentials is perhaps the lack of push and follow up from professional business management approach even for survival, leave alone a growth strategy. Besides any action of turnaround or restructuring are considered detrimental to the government in ensuring success at the ballot box. Alternatively these are considered as potential opportunities to generate revenues for the government in terms of disinvestments and collecting huge funds for revenue generation targets to meet the government's budgetary commitments.

The speed of technological disruption in telecom industry is perhaps the severest amongst all industries in India and also in global markets. While private organizations are aware of the impact of disruptive technological changes, the Government is not very sure of meeting such challenges by concerned PSUs. Hence, allowing technological obsolescence

Indian Business Case Studies. Priti Pachpande and Sham Bachhav, Oxford University Press. © ASM Group of Institutes, Pune, India 2022. DOI: 10.1093/oso/9780192869401.003.0018

to worsen the distressing situations at PSUs such as BSNL has rendered the unit to be put on the list of sick units.

Revival of the Sick?

Bharat Sanchar Nigam Limited (BSNL) officers' group has warned that things may go out of hand, and the state-controlled telco would not survive for long unless the central government takes a decision on the telco's revival and facilitates a soft loan for capital as well as operational expenses.

'The situation is worsening and if a decision is not taken by the PMO, and a soft loan is not provided to meet Capex and Opex, BSNL will not last long. We have already apprised the concerned in Central Government of the situation,' said Sanchar Nigam Executives Association (SNEA) President Aftab Ahmad Khan. Khan further said that the BSNL officers have informed the country's top office about the situation which is deteriorating every passing day, and the decision-making within the government remains slow.

The Department of Telecommunications (DoT), according to him, has also not even released a credit worth Rs 3,300 crore since the Presidential Sanction it was granted back in March this year, after the delayed salary disbursement for the first time. Some of the executives' demands included allowing bank loan till the time of land monetization, allocation of 4G airwaves, and refund of access payment to the tune of Rs 2,100 crore.

The association also attributed bureaucratic hurdles leading to vendors' outstanding worth Rs 2,500 crore. More than 100 vendors including small-and-medium businesses owners agitated at BSNL Delhi headquarters 'We fully support BSNL executives' union. Since the rejuvenation plan has so far delayed, there is no option but to allow Rs 6,000 crore to bridge funding to pay to operational creditors.'

Telecom Exports Promotion Council (TEPC) Co-Chairman Sandeep Aggarwal said, adding that salary payments alone couldn't make the telco survive.

The Finance Ministry officials had opposed the VRS package worth Rs 6,365 crore to BSNL, and Rs 2,120 crore to MTNL. However, the telecom department has been working on a slew of initiatives for BSNL revival that would require a Cabinet nod.

Besides real estate assets monetization, the department is also looking to lease out towers and fibre infrastructure which, according to analysts could bring much-needed respite in the short term since land unfreeze may be dragged due to multiple policy challenges including the mutation process.

Niti Aayog, the government's policy think-tank, estimated BSNL's real estate at Rs 1 lakh crore, fibre assets at Rs. 54,000 crore and telecom towers at Rs. 29,000 crore. India's fourth-largest operator, according to industry statistics, has the lowest debt of close to Rs. 20,000 crores when compared to private sector rivals such as Vodafone Idea having Rs.1.20 lakh crores, Bharti Airtel having Rs.1.10 lakh crores, and Reliance Jio having Rs. 1.12 lakh crore worth of liabilities.

The Group of Ministers (GoM) headed by home minister discussed offering voluntary retirement scheme (VRS) and the fourth-generation or 4G airwaves to the stressed state-controlled BSNL and Mahanagar Telephone Nigam Limited (MTNL).

The sources aware of the development said that the group during the two-hour-long meeting discussed the ways to bring back the two public sector service providers back to health and considered monetization of land and building assets to fund VRS to the willing employees.

The centre is also mulling operating synergy between BSNL and MTNL, to further save operational costs. MTNL offers cellular services in two metropolitans—Delhi and Mumbai whereas BSNL operates in rest of the country.

The revenue to wage ratio of both telcos is much higher than those of private sector players. Since 2016, both public sector operators have been demanding allocation of 4G radio waves to stay competitive in the data-led service delivery which is also leading to their revenue fall on a quarter-to-quarter basis. The administrative cost for the allocation of 4G radio waves to BSNL is pegged at Rs. 14,000 crores.

The government also needs to immediately look at assets monetization strategies including towers and fibre to make BSNL stay afloat. The real estate assets, fibre optic network, and mobile towers of BSNL are pegged at Rs 1.10 lakh crore, Rs.60,000 crores, and Rs.35,000 crores tentatively.

The proceeds can further be used to fund VRS, 4G, and 5Gspectrum, as well as operational expenses of both telcos.

Bridging the Income-Expenditure Gap

Public sector BSNL is in the process of identifying land parcels all over the country for monetization, which as per its internal estimate is valued at Rs 20,000 crore in 2018–2019.

The state-run telecom major's corporate office has circulated a list of land parcels which are proposed for monetization through the Department of Investment and Public Asset Management (DIPAM) in the first instance.

Time-bound monetization of land assets, mobile towers, and fibre networks will help BSNL earn some money in these tough times of falling revenues and rising losses.

However it is understood that these land parcels are not completely free of encumbrances. 'The total area of land parcels, which are spread across the country and have in-built structures, buildings and factories, is 32.77 lakh square meters (sq. m.) and the spare able land parcel is 31.97 lakh sq. m.,' said a BSNL corporate office letter to its circles seeking their comments.

'The fair value of spare able parcel as on April 1, 2015, is Rs 17,397 crore and the estimated present fair value of these lands is Rs 20,296 crore. The enhancement in valuation is based on cost inflation index for FY 2014–15 as 240 and FY 2018–19 as 280.' The valuation of these land parcels is proposed to be done along with the structures lying in the parcel after the in-principle approval for sale or long-term lease by the government.

'The cost of buildings has not been included in the Fair Value of land parcels,' it added. BSNL telecom has factories at Mumbai, Kolkata, West Bengal, Ghaziabad, Jabalpur and wireless stations, as well as other offices and staff colonies have been included in the list of land parcels to be monetized. Some of these parcels are mutated, while some are not and the status of some of these parcels are freehold and some are on leasehold.

Struggling with poor cash flows from services and a severe financial crunch due to a huge workforce of 1.76 lakh (add 40,000 contract labour), BSNL is looking for non-core asset monetization under the broad policy of the government where DIPAM is the nodal department. BSNL is expected to post losses of over Rs 14,000 crore for the financial year 2018–2019, while its revenue is slated to be around Rs 19,308 crore. Salary expenditure is set to be a massive 75% of the firm's total expenses at Rs 14,488 crore.

Its provisional loss in 2015–2016 was Rs 4,859 crore, Rs 4,793 crore 2016–2017, and Rs 7,993 crore in 2017–2018. BSNL's loss is estimated to balloon to Rs 14,202 crore in 2018–2019.

'Low tariffs due to fierce competition in the mobile segment, high staff cost and absence of 4G services (except in few places) in the data-centric telecom market are the main reasons for losses of BSNL.

In line with sector trends, BSNL has also seen a dip in its revenue after the entry of Reliance Jio in the market in 2016. The company's revenue is pegged at around Rs 19,308 crore for 2018–2019, compared with Rs 25,071 crore in 2017–2018, and Rs 31,533 crore in 2016–2017.

Conclusions

The government is taking steps to make public sector BSNL more competitive and these include up-gradation of technology and capital infusion. BSNL has inherited legacy issues and steps are being taken to make BSNL more competitive. 'To ensure stability in the Telecom sector, one PSU is very important.' It must be noted that India has the cheapest mobile and data rates across the world.

The government is considering capital infusion, including equity infusion in the public sector telecom company.

The government is also working out introduction of 4G services, after members expressed concern over lack of technology up-gradation by BSNL. BSNL has to spend 75% of its revenues in paying salaries to employees, while private companies have very low employee cost.

BSNL has informed that there is no proposal to lay off over 54,000 employees. As per TRAI report the total market share of BSNL is 10.72% as on 31 March 2019, including 9.96% in mobile wireless technology. However, stiff competition in mobile segment, high employee cost, and absence of 4G services (except in few places for BSNL in the data-centric telecom market) is adversely affecting the competitive strength of BSNL.

Case Questions

1. Do you think the current situation at BSNL is because of lack of business acumen in running such companies in perennial distress?

2. How do you suggest the Government clears its dubious distinction of treating ailing units as cash cows for disinvestment rather than as successful businesses?

3. Do you see any turnaround strategy workable for BSNL? What areas do you think the Government should focus to avoid closure of PSUs such as BSNL and Air India?

19

Future of the 'Future Group'

A Case Study on an E-commerce Retail—The Giant 'Future Group'

Learning Objectives

The present study is devoted to search for the probable causes of the financial crises faced by the conglomerate group. The study is intended to learn the areas where the decisions of the retail tycoon went wrong and the effect of inappropriate decisions on the organization. The study also highlights the present condition and the corona effect on the organization. This is probably the best example of ineffectual handling of finances, indecent assessment of financial and business risk and erroneous as well inconsistent portfolio management.

Synopsis

To be, or not to be. the Hamletian dilemma has often dogged Future Group founder and CEO Kishore Biyani. He has often been candid about his ambitious plans, but hasn't been able to walk the talk so far. Biyani's announcements about his new ventures and exits from the existing ones, apart from fundraising to fuel future expansion, have only one thing in common—remarkable inconsistency.

The Case Study

Rewrite Rules, Retain Values is the principle with which Kishore Biyani the founder of the Future Group has started his entrepreneurial journey in the 1980s in Mumbai.

Indian Business Case Studies. Priti Pachpande and Sham Bachhav, Oxford University Press. © ASM Group of Institutes, Pune, India 2022. DOI: 10.1093/oso/9780192869401.003.0019

Today the Future group, a conglomerate company is handling a wide portfolio of brands in Food, FMCG, and Fashion, pioneering country's modern retail network. In retail sector the company has brands like Big Bazar, FBB, Central, and Nilgiris. Tasty Treat, Golden Harvest, Karmiq, Kara, Sunkist, ThinkSkin, Mother Earth, Kosh, Nilgiris are among the leading brands in food sector from the Future Group.

The flagship company of Future Group, Future Retail Ltd. W5 was incorporated in 2007. The company has developed presence across India with approximately 50 million customer base as of March 2019. Kishore Biyani was called as father of Indian Retail Sector. With such a glorious background, what went wrong to an extent that the group is now in financial distress, is the problem statement of this case study.

According to Soumya Gupta, the trademark of Future Group is rapid, inorganic growth. In the last decade, Future Group has mutated considerably through a stream of acquisitions, sales, and spin-offs. Year-on-year comparisons have become so difficult that most analysts tracking the group's five listed entities have stopped coverage.

His take on e-commerce and speciality retail has wavered. The ambitious plan to sell a 10% stake in Future Group to a foreign portfolio investor (media reports say it is Amazon) has not materialized. However, Biyani's grandstanding has helped. Dalal Street investors have bet on Future Group's listed companies despite their tepid growth and mounting debt. But institutional investors have been circumspect.

Biyani, the face of Future Group, hasn't given up on his ambitious plans. He wants to make it the largest retailer in India (now Reliance Retail). He has been piloting a restructuring exercise in various group companies for over three years. It is aimed at growing the top line and bottom line, improving margins, and, most important, reducing debt. This exercise has attracted media attention and sparked off speculation about Biyani's next move. But in reality, Biyani's efforts are neither easing his retail, consumer, and lifestyle businesses, nor jump-starting growth.

Debt Financing and Restructuring

After tasting success with Big Bazaar, Biyani diversified into other businesses such as financial services, formal clothes retailing and insurance. In 2012, Biyani sold his Pantaloon brand to Aditya Birla group for Rs 1,600 crore. Pantaloon was the first brand started by Biyani way back in 1987. The deal was to help Biyani reduce the group's debt of Rs 7,850 crore.

Later, he acquired a series of retail brands—neighbourhood format stores Easyday, supermarket chain Nilgiris, Heritage Foods' retail operations, grocery-stores chain Sangam Direct, premium hypermarkets chain Hypercity, and Foodworld Supermarkets. He was reportedly in talks to acquire Spencer's Retail's More (the deal went to a Samara Capital-Amazon joint venture in September 2018).

Biyani's debt is embedded in a holding company, Future Corporate Resources Pvt Ltd, which is controlled by several family-owned limited liability partnerships (LLPs).

Until April 2017, Future Corporate Resources was not the main group entity. Earlier, Biyani used a larger number of entities to raise funds and control his businesses. An important entity in that network was Suhani Trading and Investment Consultants. Suhani itself remained overburdened by debt.

Biyani raised INR3,000 crore in December 2018 from three investors—AION Capital, its insurance JV partner Generali Group, and its shoe-brand JV partner Skechers (both partners bought more equity in their respective JVs). Biyani said it was to reduce debt. Besides, Future Retail got INR 2,000 crore equity from its promoter Future Group to 'completely do away with lease rentals in the next 18 months', the company said in a BSE filing. Clearly, settling debt tops Biyani's priority list. But Future Group's group entities are not cash rich. In FY18, Future Corporate Resources had only INR20.6 crore of cash and cash equivalents, down from INR80 crore in FY17. But in FY18, the company had INR 613.56 crore of finance costs to cover.

Biyani needs to improve the profitability of his businesses to stay on the radar of investors. It'll help fund his aggressive business plans. ET

Prime put his three main businesses under the lens. FMCG arm Future Consumer Ltd has yet to make an annual profit, as per Reuters Eikon data. In FY18, the company made a net loss of INR 26 crore. Future Lifestyle Fashions and Future Retail, though profitable, operated on slender margins (2.8% and 0.6% in FY18).

However, the numbers are improving, as data from the first three-quarters of FY19 show. But the group has some catching up to do with rivals on key performance ratios, including enterprise value to sales and price-to-sales per share. Still, these three group companies trade at much higher multiples than their performing peers.

Inconsistent Approach

Biyani has kept Future Group in the news every month since 2016. For instance, Future Group remained in the news last year after Biyani disclosed plans to sell a 10% stake in the company to a foreign portfolio investor. Shares of the listed group companies surged on speculation that the investor was Amazon. There were media reports later that the deal had fallen through because the government changed rules for foreign direct investment in e-commerce, hurting Amazon's business prospects, in December 2018.

Since then, the Future Group stock has fallen, but it is still relatively more expensive than its peers. Future Retail is trading around INR80 below its 200-day simple moving average (SMA). Similarly, Future Consumer is around INR 4 below its 200-day SMA. Only Future Lifestyle is trading above the 200-day SMA, close to its 52-week high. Many of these statements had a discernible impact on the share prices of the three listed companies.

It perhaps explains why institutional investors have been wary of the Future Group. Future Retail had just 3.45% of their shares with domestic mutual funds until December 2017. Foreign investors together hold less than 10% in the company. Future Lifestyle has just 1.1% of its stock with domestic mutual funds, but it managed to sell 10% of its stake to LVMH Moët Hennessy.

Louis Vuitton, the luxury goods conglomerate, for an undisclosed amount in May 2018. Meanwhile, the enterprise value of these companies, a measure of the company's total value (market capitalization plus total debt minus cash and cash equivalents) has remained largely flat over the past couple of years.

What Next?

For now, Biyani is tiding over his debt worries with funds from myriad sources. Apart from the INR 3,000 crore raised this year, he also raised INR 1,700 crore from Premji Invest, the family office of Wipro founder Azim Premji, for a 6% stake in Future Retail in June last year. Now, after promoters put their own money into Future Retail, everyone is waiting for the planned 10% stake sale.

Financing debt is now hurting the businesses. In a recent earnings note, equities-brokerage firm Jefferies pointed out that Future Retail's profit after tax came in lower than expected because interest expenses grew unexpectedly, almost 1.5 times quarter on quarter. Even Future Lifestyle, the best of the lot in terms of stock performance saw a 16% rise in interest cost in the December quarter year on year. This was at a time when the company was spending on the expansion of its Brand Factory store network in a relatively lower-margin format. So, where will Biyani rustle up the funding for his big plans from? Let him *talk*. Hopefully, next time he will walk it.

The Covid-19 Effect

How Loan Moratorium and IBC Saved Kishore Biyani from Debt Crisis

Government's stimulus measures turned out to be a blessing in disguise for Kishore Biyani, the father of India's modern retailing. Reserve Bank of India (RBI)'s loan moratorium and the suspension of Insolvency and Bankruptcy Code (IBC) have come at just the right time for Biyani's Future Group companies, saving him from a major debt crisis.

Fortunately for Biyani, since IBC is suspended for a year, even if he defaults, lenders will not be able to recommend the companies for insolvency. Instead, the loans will have to be restructured. 'The banks will not be able to take the loan defaulting companies for insolvency during this period. It will force the bankers to restructure the loans of Future group companies,' said a banker.

However the pandemic has disrupted the operations of Future Group companies. The group was completely dependent on cash flow of companies to pay off debts. The flagship company Future Retail had posted a consolidated profit of Rs 165 crore in the third quarter of last financial year.

Conclusions

According to industry sources, Future Group's financials are under severe stress. 'Only a quick sale can save his empire from defaulting on loans,' says a Mumbai-based investment banker. Biyani is struggling to complete the sale of a major portion of his retail assets. To avoid defaults he needs to do it before August, when EMI moratorium ends. If he does not sell the assets, he will not be able to make loan repayments with interest that run into hundreds of crores, say banking sources.

Credit rating agency Icra Ltd is the lead agency that rates debt issued by FCRL. As of 16 January this year, it had ratings for five debt instruments issued by the company, amounting to a total of Rs 1,400 crores. All of them are rated BBB-, meaning they carry a 'moderate degree of risk' of defaulting on outstanding obligations. The outlook on this rating is stable as per the January report. Each tranche of FCRL's long-term loans has remained at a BBB- rating since June 2012.

The rapid inorganic growth with inconsistent business decisions is the causes of the financial distress of the Future Group. In the last decade, Future Group has mutated considerably through a stream of acquisitions, sales, and spin-offs. Year-on-year comparisons have become so difficult that most analysts tracking the group's five listed entities have stopped coverage.

Case Questions

1. Is it the conglomerate diversification that hamper the success of the Future Group?

2. Is it the inorganic growth the only cause of the collapse of giant?

3. What corrective measures should have been taken by Biyani to safeguard his business empire?

20
ITC at Cross Roads

As a new generation of leaders take guard at ITC Ltd, the Kolkata-based multi-business house finds itself in the throes of a strange paradox. Its glorious past, and present, cast a shadow over its future. Its two distinct business areas—cigarettes on one hand, and packaged foods, personal care products, apparel, hotels, and information technology on the other—pull in different directions. The sales of the former, despite being tagged sin products, have made it the country's fifth most valuable listed company, while the latter, notwithstanding growth over the years, have been a persistent drag on profits.

The trouble for ITC, incorporated in 1910 as Imperial Tobacco Company of India Ltd, is that tobacco is an ageing business, a legacy of its past, albeit one which has driven its success. The others—foods, personal care products, hotels—offer different economics but seem to be its manifest future. Unfortunately, it is a future in which there is no real visibility of any meaningful profits.

There is no questioning ITC's stellar performance: between 1995–1996 and 2015–2016, its compound annual growth rate, or CAGR, of gross revenue was 12%, while its consolidated return on capital employed was 45.2%. Post-tax profit over this period was 19.9%, while its market cap went up from Rs.5,571 crore to Rs.2.64 trillion. Even after 106 years, its cigarettes business is a slot machine that keeps throwing out cash by the bucketful.

Yet, the very success of the cigarettes business has for years masked the failures of its many ventures into other areas where the returns have been abysmal. It hasn't been for lack of ambition though.

At its last annual general meeting, outgoing chairman Yogi. C. Deveshwar, who has helmed the company for the past two decades, announced a sales target for the consumer business of Rs.1 trillion by 2030

Indian Business Case Studies. Priti Pachpande and Sham Bachhav, Oxford University Press. © ASM Group of Institutes, Pune, India 2022. DOI: 10.1093/oso/9780192869401.003.0020

from Rs.9,704 crore in FY16. For that to happen, the business would have to grow at a CAGR of 18%. That's a stiff target, but not an impossible one.

What will test the mettle of Sanjiv Puri, Deveshwar's likely successor after being named chief operating officer (COO) last month, will be getting the consumer business to contribute significantly to profits. In the June quarter, of the total segment profit of Rs.3,486 crore, cigarettes contributed Rs.3,005 crore, while the non-tobacco consumer business reported a loss of Rs.4.5 crore. In 2015–2016, however, it did report a profit of Rs.70.5 crore.

Hotels, Branded Foods

The fact is, ITC has been in investment mode forever. Its first Indian chairman, Ajit Haksar, led a massive investment surge into hotels in the 1970s, as a way of de-risking the cigarettes business. Even the turning point in Deveshwar's career at ITC came when in 1984 he was inducted into ITC's board of directors, taking charge of Welcomgroup (hotel division) as its chairman and kicking off his ascent by building flagship hotels in Delhi and Mumbai. Yet, despite over 100 properties in its stable now, that business is still not majorly profitable. Its branded foods business, which began in 2001 with the launch of its 'Kitchens of India' ready-to-eat Indian dishes, followed by Mint-o and Candyman confectionery and Aashirvaad *atta* (wheat flour), is also nearly 15 years old, while the personal care business started in 2005.

An earlier analysis of segment-wise data for the company since FY03 showed that of the increase in profits between then and FY16, cigarettes contributed 84.4%, paper 5.9%, and hotels only 0.4%. The consumer goods business contributed 1.7%, despite accounting for 31.3% of incremental sales in this 13-year period, and is now more than half the size of the cigarettes business.

Through the years, ITC's focus has been on achieving scale in these businesses, which it has done. But profitability hasn't kept pace with sales growth. In the 13-year period, the consumer goods business has reported slender segment profits in only the past two years. All this didn't matter till cigarettes continued to grow, and ITC's massive 80% market share ensured it creamed the bulk of the profits. That party has now been broken up by a number of factors, with health-related issues forcing governments everywhere to come down hard on the tobacco industry.

Stubbing It Out

ITC can't even fight that stigma anymore as there is overwhelming evidence to suggest cigarettes are a silent killer. The World Health Organization (WHO) has estimated that nearly a million Indians die each year of tobacco-related causes though ITC's cigarettes are only one among the several culprits, including bidis and chewing tobacco. That's prompted the government to run an aggressive anti-smoking campaign, leading to a decline in smoking.

In the year ended December, cigarette sales in India dropped to 88.1 billion sticks—a 15-year low and a decline of 8.2% from 95.9 billion sticks sold in 2014, according to a Euromonitor study. Cigarette sales by volume have been declining since 2011. The drop in 2015 was the steepest, the study added. While some say the decline may be accounted for by counterfeit cigarettes, it is quite clear there is to be no more growth in this business. The last time ITC's cigarettes volume grew was in the fourth quarter of FY13, according to an HDFC Securities Ltd report.

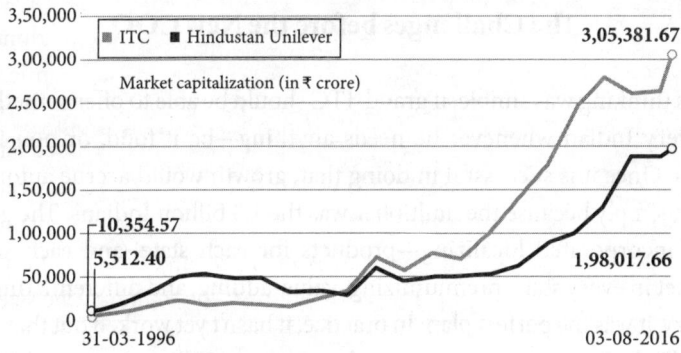

Racing Ahead

Shares of ITC pulled away from those of Hindustan Unilever in 2005 and have never looked back since.

To his credit, outgoing chairman Deveshwar has been cognizant of this and raised the flag in his annual general meeting speech 16 years ago when he announced: 'ITC's strategic thrust is founded on its ability to continuously invest in existing and new capabilities.

As a result, one of ITC's most important assets today is its pool of diverse core competencies residing in its various businesses. The governance structure has been so designed as to place it in a position to pursue new avenues of growth without diluting the focus on its existing lines of business.'

Deveshwar embarked on the onerous task of transforming ITC from a cigarette maker to a packaged consumer goods company around 2000. Since then, he has stormed into the bastion of redoubtable players such as Hindustan Unilever Ltd, Procter and Gamble Home Products Ltd, Pepsi Foods Pvt. Ltd, Britannia Industries Ltd, Nestle India Ltd, and Parle Agro Pvt. Ltd, with varying rates of success.

In his 2010 rolling five-year plan, he declared he wanted the consumer products business to grow to Rs.12,000 crore by 2015 even as the firm aimed for sales of Rs.55,000 crore. In fiscal 2016, ITC clocked Rs.9,731 crore in revenue from sales of food and personal care products, and made a pre-tax profit of Rs.70.5 crore from the segment. So, it isn't quite there yet, though gross revenue did cross Rs.50,000 crore during the year.

The Challenges before the New COO

ITC's thinking was simple, if grand. ITC should be able to offer something to every Indian whenever he needs anything—be it food, or non-food items. Once it is successful in doing that, growth would accrue automatically, simply because the multiplier was the 1.3 billion Indians. The game plan incorporated localizing—products for each state, and each small market in every state; premiumizing, value-adding, and differentiating. In theory, it was the perfect plan. In practice, it hasn't yet worked out that way. For all efforts, the newer businesses haven't been pulling their weight.

Enter Sanjiv Puri, the man on track to succeed him. How Puri, an Indian Institute of Technology-Kanpur alumnus who joined ITC in 1986, will get the dog to wag the tail is going to be a fascinating challenge. He has had the experience, having moved around the company he started his career with. Before taking over as COO, he was responsible for over-seeing the consumer goods, paperboards, paper and packaging, and agri-businesses. His experience base cuts across verticals as well as functions, including business leadership positions in manufacturing, operations, and information technology.

His challenges are daunting. The dynamics of the hotel industry are such that sustained profitability is almost a mirage. In foods, the company, along with its peers, faces a formidable new competitor in yoga guru Baba Ramdev's Patanjali. Also has to brood over the business opportunities the company may have missed over the years.

Thus, it was one of the earliest companies in India to build an efficient and substantive digital platform in the form of eChaupal. But with the e-commerce revolution happening, it hasn't been able to leverage that into tangible gains for any of its businesses, including foods and consumer products.

One way is to pull in some additional muscle is by tapping the resource base of the £13 billion British American Tobacco Plc. (BAT), which holds nearly 30% of the Indian company. This could be done by leveraging the expertise of R.E. Lerwill, who has represented Tobacco Manufacturers (India) Ltd, a subsidiary of BAT, on the ITC board since November 2013. Lerwill, who has in the past been executive director of Cable and Wireless Plc. as well as group finance director of WPP Group Plc., was responsible for developing and managing major international businesses in both companies.

BAT has played a very little role in the affairs of the firm it set up. It is an arrangement that brought peace to the troubled Indian company in that stormy period in the mid-1990s, and has also allowed it to frame an altogether Indian narrative for its growth.

Lessons from BAT

ITC could draw lessons from how BAT divested several non-core businesses it had got into over time, only to emerge sharper and stronger. In the 1970s, its US retail division, then called BATUS Retail Group, acquired Gimbels, Kohl's, and Saks Fifth Avenue. It also bought Marshall

Field's and its divisions in 1982 as well as the UK retail chain Argos in 1979. Soon, however, it realized that returns on these diversifications were low as compared with those in its cigarette business. Consequently, Saks Fifth Avenue, Kohl's grocery stores as well as Marshall Field's were all sold off, while Gimbels was closed down. Subsequent to these sales, it is now focused almost exclusively on cigarettes, where it is among the market leaders.

Indeed, far from going away, tobacco may be more resilient than is commonly believed. Perhaps, even with the elements stacked against it, tobacco is still the best investment bet for ITC.

According to a 2015 Credit Suisse report, since the beginning of 2005, the MSCI Global Tobacco Index has risen 196.4%, providing an 11% annual return. It far outperformed the catch-all MSCI World Index, which went up 50.6% in the same period. Not surprisingly, tobacco is a perennial winner in the markets: a dollar invested in the US market in 1900 in tobacco, gave an annualized return of 14.6%, and a terminal value of $6.2 million by 2015.

'Vice' stocks tend to do well in good times as well as bad, and ITC, without the burden of its other investments, is among the best of those stocks, given its dominant market position and its huge cash hoard. Shrugging aside the plethora of social strictures, the industry is continuing to innovate. According to a Bloomberg Intelligence report, the industry's latest innovation is 'heat not burn' devices. A 'heat not burn' vaporizer heats ground tobacco leaves and delivers a nicotine hit to the user without producing much smoke or ashes. Early experimenters were smaller firms; but now, bigger companies such as Philip Morris and Reynolds 'have made it clear they're intent on catching up'.

For years, ITC has poured money to buy market share in the personal care business. But throwing cash is never a sustainable strategy. So far, it has always countered the drop in cigarette sales volume by expanding revenue through price hikes. Now, however, it faces the classic dilemma of the smoker who knows smoking is killing him but can't kick the habit because the process is painful.

Case Questions

1. How long can ITC continue to depend on its tobacco products division in spite of skyrocketing taxes and anti-tobacco movements. Is this ethically a correct strategy to produce since the customer wants its products irrespective of severe health hazards?

2. How do you rate the chances of the marketing strategy of ITC to succeed amidst global giants such Kellogs, McDonalds' and many more and the very Indian Patanjali products?

3. Could you suggest a long-term growth and sustainability strategy for ITC based product and business diversification models.